T0270064

THE
FUTURE
BUILT BY
WOMEN

THE FUTURE BUILT BY WOMEN

CREATING A BRIGHTER TOMORROW THROUGH TECH AND INNOVATION

BROOKE MARKEVICIUS

WILEY

For general information on our other products and services or for technical support, please contact our Customer Care Department within the United States at (800) 762-2974, outside the United States at (317) 572-3993 or fax (317) 572-4002.

Wiley also publishes its books in a variety of electronic formats. Some content that appears in print may not be available in electronic formats. For more information about Wiley products, visit our web site at www.wiley.com.

Library of Congress Cataloging-in-Publication Data

Names: Markevicius, Brooke, author.
Title: The future built by women / Brooke Markevicius.
Description: Hoboken, New Jersey : Wiley, [2024] | Includes index.
Identifiers: LCCN 2023053434 (print) | LCCN 2023053435 (ebook) | ISBN 9781394218554 (cloth) | ISBN 9781394218578 (adobe pdf) | ISBN 9781394218561 (epub)
Subjects: LCSH: Businesswomen. | Women in technology.
Classification: LCC HD6053 .M344 2024 (print) | LCC HD6053 (ebook) | DDC 658.1/1082—dc23/eng/20231221
LC record available at https://lccn.loc.gov/2023053434
LC ebook record available at https://lccn.loc.gov/2023053435

Cover Design: Wiley
Cover Image: © youarehere/Adobe Stock Photos
SKY10068702_030124

To the matriarch of our family, my dear Nanee Dickens. You showed me what it meant to work hard for your dreams. You were the ultimate energizer bunny and built a future for you and your family. You were a lover of books and writing and even though you did not get a book published, I got us one. Thanks for visiting me often as a beautiful red cardinal outside my window as I wrote the pages in this book.

To my daughter, the future will be brighter because you will be one of the women building it. You are so strong and smart. Your creativity and curiosity will get you far. Your writing inspires me, and I know one day you will be publishing a book, too.

Contents

Foreword

As I REFLECT on my journey through the tech world—from the early days at Facebook to my ventures in investing and exploring the realms of web3—I am continuously inspired by the unyielding pursuit of innovation and the essential role of uplifting women in this sector. It's this very spirit that makes *The Future Built by Women*, authored by the extraordinary Brooke Markevicius, so resonant with me.

Brooke and I share more than just a passion for pioneering in technology; we are kindred spirits in balancing the demands of motherhood with the relentless drive of building companies and shaping careers. This shared bond, along with our love for running, a discipline that has sharpened our resilience and grit, are threads that Brooke masterfully intertwines throughout her book.

My experiences at Facebook, witnessing the whirlwind of innovation, coupled with my ongoing involvement in web3, have deepened my belief in the crucial role of women in tech. Brooke's insights in *The Future Built by Women* powerfully mirror this conviction, offering a narrative that is both personal and universal.

This book stands as a pragmatic compass for women charting their course in tech entrepreneurship. It emphasizes the importance of resilience, education, mindset, and strong support systems essential for navigating not just the industry's challenges but also the diverse personal commitments and aspirations that each woman brings to her unique journey.

Running the New York City Marathon this year was a reaffirmation of the parallels between the endurance required in long-distance running and the tenacity needed in tech and business—a sentiment echoed in Brooke's authentic and compelling narrative.

The Future Built by Women is more than a manual; it is an inspiration for women harboring grand ambitions in technology and in making a positive impact on the world. Brooke's journey of becoming "dangerously skilled" in tech and her blueprint for entrepreneurial success deeply resonate with my own path, from the early days at Facebook to my current endeavors in tech investments and the exploration of web3.

This book is not just a compilation of advice; it heralds a future where women are the creators and trailblazers of technological and societal progress. Prepare to be inspired, educated, and empowered to be part of shaping this new era.

Consider *The Future Built by Women* as your marathon—a testament to the remarkable achievement's women can attain when they harness their passion, purpose, and vision in the world of tech and entrepreneurship.

Randi Zuckerberg

Introduction: A Vision for the Future Built by Women

IMAGINE A WORLD where technology and innovation are guided by diverse perspectives, where creativity and ingenuity are not hindered by gender boundaries, and women play an instrumental role in shaping the future. This is a future focused not on building for the sake of technology but for the sake of humanity, where real issues are met with innovative solutions. As a woman and a mother, I see how far we have yet to go to realize this vision, yet I fervently believe we must articulate, champion, and work collectively toward this future; otherwise, it will remain a mere aspiration.

When I began building my company, Allobee, I spoke about it ceaselessly. I shared its mission and vision with anyone willing to listen. The power in this lay in the resonance it evoked in others. Whether they joined as followers, clients, freelancers, team members, or investors, they wanted to be part of a mission addressing a critical issue: the future of work for women. With 43% of women leaving the workforce before the pandemic and an additional two million during, it was evident that the conventional model of work was failing women. I knew that unless women participated in designing the future of work, we would continue to be left out.

My journey showed me that I was not alone. Women were at the forefront, building companies to tackle major societal issues, from childcare to infertility, work-life balance to bias in AI, and unpaid labor. These women, many of them mothers, were motivated by the belief that solving these problems would create a better future for their children. A recent *Wall Street Journal* article highlighted that 78% of Americans lack confidence that their children's generation will have a better life than their own (https://www.wsj.com/articles/most-americans-doubt-their-children-will-be-better-off-wsj-norc-poll-finds-35500ba8). Such a reality may seem bleak, but instead of wallowing in it, I choose to make a difference. I choose to build, each day, contributing in small but significant ways toward creating better and more impactful solutions. I am convinced that our empathy as women; our intrinsic drive to solve problems that affect us, our families, and our communities; make us potent builders.

Given the right tools, such as coding or cutting-edge technologies like artificial intelligence, I believe we women can revolutionize the world. We can build a world that instills confidence in the future for our children.

However, my path to this understanding was not linear. I wasn't exposed to the world of technology or building until after a career in nonprofit. I am a firm believer that everyone has the potential to build if they tap into what I call the GEMS framework. In the pages to come, I will share how I transitioned into the world of technology. So, if you're questioning whether you're on the right career path to shape the future, I encourage you to keep reading.

PART

I

The GEMS Framework

1

Tech for Good

I RECALL THE moment that sparked my interest in technology with vivid clarity. My eyes were glued to the screen as I watched a team set up technology centers in developing countries, teaching women to code and offering them a newfound sense of freedom. This was not a documentary or an inspirational feature; it was a video my husband was showing me about the new initiatives at his company, Microsoft. For the first time, I was confronted with the idea that technology could be used as a force for good, and it radically changed my perspective.

Growing up as the daughter of a preacher and a teacher, my career path had always seemed clear. I was raised to value service and servant leadership, so I naturally gravitated toward roles in teaching or nonprofit work. After graduating college, I served as a missionary for the United Methodist Church's US-2 Missionary program, later transitioning into nonprofit management.

Until the moment I saw that video, I had believed that service-focused professions were the only avenues to bring about positive change in the world. However, that video challenged my preconceptions. I saw a tech company using technology not

3

merely for its own advancement, but to make a tangible difference in people's lives.

At that time, I was feeling rather burnt out from nonprofit work and was seeking a new direction. Ironically, I was in grad school pursuing a master's in social work, but I was frustrated by the requirement of unpaid internships and the demanding work hours. Deep down, I craved something new.

I considered what I already knew about technology: I was the go-to tech helper at every nonprofit I had worked for, I had built simple websites for side hustles and other nonprofits, and my husband, a computer science major working at Microsoft, could guide me. Weighing the pros and cons of a career pivot, the advantages quickly tipped the scales.

Within a week, I applied for a master's program in computer information systems at Boston University, leaving my MSW program behind. It was time to venture into the world of tech, and I was determined to use it for the greater good.

Embracing a new career path might have been daunting, but I've always had a penchant for change. Whether it's my ADHD compelling me to seek variety or my childhood experiences of frequently moving and adapting, I've never shied away from transformation. However, when I truly believe in something, I go all in, which is exactly what happened when I dove headfirst into my new career in tech. I reveled in the novelty, invigorated by this awakening to an entirely new world.

Recalling a story my father frequently shared in his sermons, I thought of my sister's wide-eyed wonder at seeing Niagara Falls for the first time. The adult visitors walked by, but as a child, she paused, awestruck by the frozen mist and water. That sense of wonder fuels curiosity, and curiosity drives innovation. Being introduced to the world of technology was my moment of wide-eyed wonder as an adult.

My newfound tech skills offered an expansive vista of possibilities. Having worked directly with children with severe emotional issues, homeless women and children, and women fleeing domestic violence, I brought a unique lens to technology. I had seen firsthand that donations and scant nonprofit funding alone were not sufficient to solve societal issues; innovative approaches were required.

Although I was unsure of exactly what I wanted to build at that time, the image of the video remained etched in my mind. The idea of using technology to help those in dire need of economic support was deeply appealing to me. It was a cause I was ready to commit to, and this marked the beginning of my journey into the world of technology.

Where Are All the Women: The Stark Reality of Women in Technology

As I delved into the world of technology, a question kept reverberating in my mind: where were all the women? As I consumed episode after episode of popular business podcast host, Guy Raz's *How I Built This*, I noticed a significant lack of female voices. This lack was perplexing and disheartening. Were other women, like me, simply unaware of technology's potential to effect positive change?

The statistics on women in technology or women building start-ups made for grim reading. Women constitute half of the US workforce, yet only 27% of them are STEM workers, according to the US Census (https://www.census.gov/library/stories/2021/01/women-making-gains-in-stem-occupations-but-still-underrepresented.html). In university computer science programs, women comprise merely about 18% of graduates.

One of my employees shared her experience of entering a computer science program years ago in Texas, only to be dissuaded by a professor who told her that it was not a place for women, and she would not succeed. She exited that path, a decision she has always regretted. Today, only 25% of computing roles are held by women, and the numbers plummet even further for women of color (https://builtin.com/women-tech/women-in-tech-workplace-statistics).

In the sphere of entrepreneurship, despite studies demonstrating that companies with diverse leadership yield higher returns, only 2% of venture capital funding goes to female-founded companies (https://techcrunch.com/2023/01/18/women-founded-startups-raised-1–9-of-all-vc-funds-in-2022-a-drop-from-2021/). These systemic barriers stifle women's abilities to scale their businesses and bring innovative solutions to the market.

At present, we're witnessing major advancements in artificial intelligence (AI), making it even more crucial to address the underrepresentation of women in the field. From hackathons to AI-based companies and discussions on AI, women are conspicuously absent.

One critical issue in the realm of AI is the inherent bias in algorithms and data, which can inadvertently perpetuate stereotypes and reinforce existing inequalities. An example can be seen in ChatGPT's language generation. It often chooses the word *empower* when prompted to write about The Riveter, a female-focused company, but opts for words like *strength* and *power* when prompted to write about a male-focused brand. This stark contrast underscores the importance of diverse voices, including women, in writing code and curating data.

We still have a long way to go, but we must be at the center of this space to build a more equitable future. How do we construct a future when women are absent from decision-making rooms or the literal coding that shapes our world?

As a mother, I've strived to expose my daughter to a world of possibilities. I bought her the Rebel Girls series as soon as it was released and have curated a library of books featuring female innovators, explorers, and scientists. I never want her to question "Where are all the women?" and hope she steps into a computer science class populated by a majority of female students.

Women have been trailblazers in technology, from Ada Lovelace, who wrote the first computer program more than 150 years ago, to Mira Murati, the current CTO of OpenAI. They have made industry-changing advancements, yet many of their stories remain untold or underappreciated.

As a graduate student, I volunteered with The Women in Technology Association in Washington, DC, mentoring high school girls interested in technology. I learned so much from this experience and witnessed the barriers these young girls still faced. Many were not being encouraged or presented with opportunities related to computer science.

Fortunately, organizations such as Girls Who Code, Code.org and Kode with Klossy have emerged to support high school and college girls interested in coding. They have done incredible work, and the statistics reflect this progress: there has been a ten-fold growth in female participation in AP Computer Science classes in just six years (https://code.org/about/2019#:~:text= One%20measure%20of%20this%20movement,org's%20 work%20alone).

In this book, I will share stories of contemporary women shaping the future of technology, including interviews with founders and women in tech. These women are tirelessly working to construct a brighter future for women in technology, reminding us all that this is a collective effort.

I am excited to introduce you to five extraordinary women who have not only left an indelible mark on the world of technology but also have inspired future generations of female innovators, including myself, which is why I like to call them the fabulous five.

Ada Lovelace: The Queen of Code

When it comes to the world's first computer programmer, it's not a man, but the queen of code, Ada Lovelace. A mathematical prodigy, Lovelace collaborated with Charles Babbage on his revolutionary analytical engine. Her visionary insights into the potential of machines to process more than just numbers laid the groundwork for modern computing. I have a picture of her in my office to remind me that women pioneered coding.

Grace Hopper: The Compiler Queen

Grace Hopper, a United States Navy rear admiral, was no ordinary computer scientist. As one of the first programmers of the Harvard Mark I computer, she was a force to be reckoned with. Hopper pioneered the development of COBOL, one of the earliest high-level programming languages, and introduced the concept of machine-independent programming languages, leading to the creation of compilers. COBOL is still around today and, fun fact, my neighbor (a woman!) is one of the only people around who still knows the language.

Hedy Lamarr: The Glamorous Inventor

Hedy Lamarr, a film actress by profession, was also a brilliant inventor with a passion for problem-solving. During World War II, Lamarr codeveloped a frequency-hopping spread spectrum communication system to protect radio-controlled torpedoes from being intercepted. Little did she know that her groundbreaking invention would form the basis of modern Wi-Fi, Bluetooth, and GPS technologies. These are technologies that now society uses daily.

Katherine Johnson: The Space Race Virtuoso

As an African American mathematician, Katherine Johnson defied racial and gender barriers at NASA to make history. Her impeccable calculations were critical to the success of the first US-crewed spaceflights, including Alan Shepard's *Freedom 7* and John Glenn's *Friendship 7* missions. Johnson's remarkable achievements earned her the prestigious Presidential Medal of

Freedom in 2015. Fun fact: my great uncle worked at NASA at the same time Katherine did.

Radia Perlman: The Mother of the Internet

Radia Perlman, a computer scientist and network engineer, played a pivotal role in shaping the internet as we know it today. As the inventor of the spanning tree protocol (STP), Perlman made it possible for Ethernet networks to expand, paving the way for large-scale networks. Her transformative work earned her the well-deserved title of the *mother of the internet*.

■ ■ ■

These five extraordinary women serve as a reminder that when it comes to shaping the future, gender is no barrier. To ensure the ongoing success of women in technology, we must invest in the potential of young girls and support their aspirations in STEM fields.

A Modern Addition

Although it's crucial to revere historical figures like the fabulous five for their contributions, it's equally important to acknowledge and find inspiration in the present-day pioneers who are actively shaping our future. A personal experience of mine illustrates this.

When you are a founder trying to navigate the world of building a company at a fast pace, you need tools that enable you to iterate at almost the speed of light. It is also helpful if the tools enable you to do a job you would usually hire for but with the tool can easily yourself. One of these tools that truly has enabled me to iterate fast is Canva. I still remember the thrill of opening Canva for the first time nearly 10 years ago. As I began to explore and play around with its features, I sensed that I was interacting with a game-changing product. What struck me immediately was its accessibility; Canva had a universal appeal that made design accessible to everyone. At its helm was cofounder and CEO, Melanie Perkins. Under her leadership, Canva has continued to democratize design, making it an integral tool for businesses, schools, and individuals across the world.

I have been using it for over 10 years, and it has supported my freelancing, my own branding within business, the ability to get Allobee up and running fast, and keeping a digital presence. I did not need to hire a social media manager or graphic designer for a long time because I had Canva at my fingertips. I know I am not alone in my Canva obsession, and the number of founders it has helped is massive. So the technology that Melanie Perkins built has allowed thousands and thousands of founders to build and innovate, and that is a powerful use of technology for good. I have listened to just about every podcast with Melanie on it and have read a lot about Canva and its inner workings, because when you find a founder that not only builds an amazing product but also builds a successful company and company culture, you look to them for hints to how you can build better.

In my office, a quote hangs prominently behind my desk, acting as a beacon of inspiration and a powerful daily reminder for myself and everyone who joins me on a Zoom call. It's a statement from the inimitable Ruth Bader Ginsburg: "Women belong in all places where decisions are being made. It shouldn't be that women are the exception."

This quote, much like my mission, embodies the belief that women must have a seat at the decision-making table. We are not, and should never be, the exception but a vital part of the equation.

My commitment is to ensure that we no longer have to ask "Where are all the women?" because our presence in the rooms where decisions are being made will be obvious and unquestioned. For this vision to become a reality, we must continue to fight for equality and create opportunities that encourage and support women in every sector, particularly technology.

2

LEGO and GEMS

As a parent, I adore LEGO kits and curated STEM and craft boxes. Granted, my patience may fray as my kids argue over who gets to place which LEGO brick on top of the other, but ultimately, I revel in the way everything coalesces. The designers of LEGO packages are sheer geniuses—it's astonishing how each piece fits perfectly to create a dinosaur, an airplane, or even a Harry Potter castle. LEGO bricks remind me of another passion of mine—Ruby Gems. Yes, I'm comparing LEGO to a programming language, but as a mother and a programmer, allow me this delightful indulgence.

LEGO's magic resides in how individual bricks work together to conjure up something extraordinary. Alone, they might not appear exceptional, but combined, they manifest an impressive creation. This insight led me to devise my GEMS framework, an acronym for grit, education, mindset, and support. It's been the backbone of my success and the bedrock for this book.

Embarking on my programming journey later in life than most, I knew I needed every available tool at my disposal, and this is where Ruby GEMS came in. Ruby GEMS are akin to pre-built LEGO parts—they're crafted by someone else, but you can use them to construct your program. They're a godsend for programmers, saving precious time and effort, enabling them to focus on what makes their applications distinctive. Reflecting on my trajectory to selling my company, Allobee, I acknowledge that the GEMS framework was instrumental in my success.

As we venture into the chapters that follow, each focusing on an element of the GEMS framework, you'll find a recurring theme: code. It's no coincidence. Code, a system of instructions for computers, is akin to the GEMS framework: a guideline for our journey to success. Also, code has been the building block to help me build the future. In coding and life, we encounter obstacles or "bugs"— issues such as skill gaps, unproductive habits, or unclear goals.

Much like a programmer iterates their code, the process of working through these bugs involves self-reflection, determination, and continuous improvement. Each solved issue leads to greater understanding and enhanced performance.

As you progress through this book, let the insights and shared stories catalyze your own process of debugging and refining. Remember, it's not just about fixing what's wrong but about continuously striving for better. That's how we evolve and grow.

In each chapter, you'll find a segment I've called "Code Review." This is your chance to pause, reflect, and identify any bugs in your own journey. It encourages you to be your own debugger, assessing and adapting your strategies as you build your future.

This practice of self-awareness has been indispensable in my journey as an entrepreneur and programmer, and I'm confident it can be equally beneficial for you. By iterating and improving your life and career strategies through these code reviews, you can become the master builder of your future.

The Power of a Framework: Unlocking Your Potential

Why adopt a framework? Many discussions on grit, particularly in the context of entrepreneurship, emphasize that life is a marathon, not a sprint. I never considered myself a runner until a good friend encouraged me to give it a try. I always believed I was bad at running, which led me to avoid it altogether. As a child, the idea of running a mile for the Presidential Fitness Challenge seemed dreadful, and I clung to various excuses: asthma, my family's lack of running enthusiasm, or my weight. The truth was, I never put in the effort to learn, practice, or seek the support needed to excel at running. However, I was a great tennis player because I invested time and energy into learning, practicing, and receiving support from my team and coach.

As I began running, I realized that if I had implemented a framework like GEMS earlier in my life, I could have overcome my self-doubt and excuses much sooner. My hope is that the GEMS framework offers a straightforward way for you to reflect on your life and career, regardless of where you are on your journey.

By practicing self-awareness and reflection, you can open yourself up to building the life and career you desire. Regularly reflecting on your experiences enables you to identify the "errors in the code" and understand why things may be failing. Sometimes, all you need is one small tweak to your "code" for your life or career to take off in the direction you want. The GEMS framework has not only helped me make those adjustments but also provided a strong foundation to ensure I never feel like I'm starting from scratch when life throws curveballs.

How to Use This Framework in Your Life

I have always enjoyed the wellness wheel, which is a tool for self-exploration that I was first exposed to in therapy years ago. It promotes the concept that balance is the key to well-being. The wellness wheel has seven dimensions, which include, physical, emotional, intellectual, spiritual, environmental, social, and occupational wellness. The theory is that these are all separate yet interconnected categories that contribute to reaching a balanced life. The wellness wheel offers you the ability to pause and reflect on the areas of your life and gut check where you are at a given time. Data and intuition drive my decision-making so I wanted to provide you with the opportunity to gather some data about where you are before you dive further into the GEMS framework and this book. The following assessment will enable you to get some base data. We will circle back to this at the end of the book and reflect on how you can further implement the GEMS framework to help you build the future.

Grit: On a scale of 1–10, rate your current level of perseverance and passion for long-term goals. Consider how often you push through challenges and maintain your focus despite setbacks.

1   5   10

1: I often give up when faced with challenges.

5: I sometimes push through challenges, but other times I give up.

10: I constantly push through challenges and maintain focus on my long-term goals.

Education: On a scale of 1–10, rate your commitment to learning and personal growth. Consider your pursuit of knowledge, formally (e.g., school, courses) and informally (e.g., reading, self-study).

1   5   10

1: I rarely seek out opportunities to learn new things.

5: I sometimes seek out learning opportunities, but not consistently.

10: I consistently seek out opportunities to learn and grow.

Mindset: On a scale of 1–10, rate your overall mindset. Consider your attitude toward life, your ability to maintain a positive outlook, and your belief in your ability to succeed.

1	5	10

1: I often have a negative outlook and struggle to believe in my ability to succeed.

5: My outlook varies: sometimes I'm positive, sometimes I'm negative.

10: I consistently maintain a positive outlook and believe in my ability to succeed.

Support: On a scale of 1–10, rate the level of support you have in your life. Consider the support you receive (e.g., from friends, family, mentors) and the support you give to others.

1	5	10

1: I feel I have little support in my life, and I rarely provide support to others.

5: I have some support in my life, and I sometimes provide support to others.

10: I have a strong support network, and I consistently provide support to others.

For each component, you can write down your current score in the middle of the gems in the next figure or you can use our worksheets from the website. I encourage you to color or fill in the outside blocks of the gems based on your score for each facet of the GEMS framework. There are eight sections around the outside that you can color in based on whether you answered a 1, 5, or 10, and this will give you a visual representation of how you are doing on each GEM. You can see there is a container in the middle of the GEMS. I added this because we physically and mentally can only take on so much at a time, and if we have too full of a container we will not thrive. The container is for the extra things in your life that are taking up space and affecting your GEMS. Write them in or simply shade the container to the area you feel is taken up with stuff in your life right now. This will give you a visual representation of where you're thriving and where you might need to focus more attention. Remember, the goal isn't to achieve a perfect score in every area, but to strive for balance and continual growth. I encourage you to use this activity with your team or a group of women and share your experiences in each GEMS area.

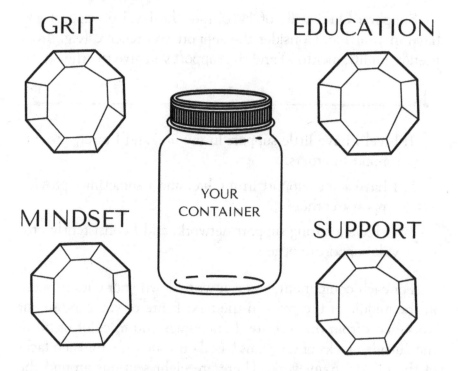

We will come back to this assessment and GEMS toward the end of the book. The upcoming chapters will delve into each element of the GEMS framework and its significance in shaping the future with women at the forefront. I have included my own experiences, as well as those of other women I've interviewed, to provide a comprehensive understanding of the GEMS framework's potential impact. My hope is that this framework, paired with real-life experiences of women building the future, will inspire and help you gain momentum to join along and help build the future.

3

The Power of Grit

Debugging Adversity, Scripting Triumph

GRIT ETYMOLOGY: DERIVED *from the Old English word* grēot, *meaning "dust, earth, or gravel," grit signifies courage and resolve, strength of character, pluck, and mettle. The word itself exudes determination and tenacity.*

Life, in many ways, is like a complex programming project. Our personalities, experiences, and individual quirks serve as the source code that dictates how we respond to challenges and seize opportunities. Some portions of this source code, such as our inherent traits, come prewritten, shaping our core disposition. However, certain crucial aspects of our code, such as grit and resilience, must be meticulously crafted, debugged, and updated over time. This ongoing process of self-development is much like the painstaking but rewarding task of coding.

In this chapter, I'll guide you through the development of your own grit module, a mental framework that embodies persistence and the will to overcome adversity. Just as any programmer learns, refines, and optimizes their coding skills, we'll delve into the strategies and approaches to developing and refining grit.

You'll discover how patience, flexibility, resilience, and self-compassion can become your core functions and how to regularly debug and optimize them for your journey.

In the spirit of learning from others, we'll also explore the life stories of remarkable women whose grit has left indelible marks on the world, offering powerful lessons to inspire and guide us. Finally, we'll conduct a code review, an introspective debugging session, to analyze the current state of your grit module and discuss potential updates to enhance its performance. Let's begin the iterative process of crafting and refining our source code for resilience, persistence, and ultimately, success.

My First Experience with True Grit

I decided to become a teacher because it was a common path in my family. Teachers were like servant leaders, and that's what we did in our home. I enjoyed history and social studies most in school because I was good at them and very interested in people and history. So, I chose to major in history for secondary education at Appalachian State University. I did well in college but often felt bored and impatient to get some real-world experience. I had been working officially since I was 15, and even babysat for extra cash since I was 12. In college, I remember wanting to be part of something bigger. But, I was a good kid, so I stayed on track with my degree and waited until graduation to see what came next.

I graduated in 2008 during the recession, and I couldn't even find a teaching job in North Carolina or Virginia. I started looking into other options because moving back home was not on the table. My dad suggested a program through the United Methodist Church that would send me to a city to do service work. After four years in the mountains, the idea of a city sounded amazing. I applied and was accepted, but they didn't tell you where you were going until a few weeks before the move.

As I drove my packed car down the mountain from college on a super foggy morning, I got a call. I pulled over, thinking it was about the placement. They told me I was going to Urbana, Illinois. My first question was "Is that a suburb of Chicago?" The program leader told me it was about 2.5 hours south of Chicago, near the University of Champaign Urbana. I finished the call politely, then sat on the side of the road in a bit of shock. They were sending me to a rural cornfield. I didn't want to go. What happened over the next few years, though, transformed me in ways I never could have imagined. Those years were some of the hardest of my life, but I learned more in them than I did in four years of college.

Moving to Illinois was my first real test of grit and resilience. I was living on my own for the first time, with no car and barely any money. I was working with kids with serious behavioral and emotional issues, in the middle of a cornfield, far away from my family and friends. The full story of those years, including a domestic violence relationship and standing in line at a food pantry, would fill another book. But, those experiences taught me more about grit and resilience than I ever wanted to know.

What I learned in those years shaped who I am today more than I realized, until I started writing this book. When you're alone and trying to find your way in life, you pick up some grit along the way. When I got that call that day, I had no idea that Illinois would give me one of the best things in my life: my husband, my best friend, and the idea for a career change. So, not everything in the cornfield turned out to be a lost cause.

Finding My Calling

During my children's fall break, I ended a call with our legal and leadership teams at my start-up. We were struggling to secure a successful funding round, and we were rapidly running out of money. Even though I'd prepared for this moment with a range of backup plans, the thought of having to close up shop was devastating. Undeterred, I decided to focus more on acquisition talks, hoping we could keep the dream alive. We were making some money but fundraising is always a tough battle, particularly for a female founder. In fall 2022, the economic situation made it even more difficult.

Running a mission-driven start-up intensifies the emotional burden. Building Allobee wasn't just about starting a business; it was about providing women with flexible work opportunities, and ensuring they were properly compensated for their efforts. Keeping Allobee afloat wasn't just about securing my own job, but providing employment for hundreds of women. My deep-seated belief in this mission gave me the grit I needed to weather this stormy period.

Angela Duckworth's book, *Grit: The Power of Passion and Perseverance*, brought the concept of grit into the limelight, especially for entrepreneurs. Her book was an instant bestseller and her TED Talk has more than 29 million views. I recall devouring the book in almost one sitting because I found it incredibly relatable. She writes, "I won't just have a job; I'll have a calling. I'll challenge myself every day. When I get knocked down, I'll get back up. I may not be the smartest person in the room, but I'll strive to be the grittiest." This struck a chord with me and I recognized grit as a key pillar in my journey of building the company and life I desired. Duckworth continues, "there are no shortcuts to excellence. Developing real expertise, figuring out really hard problems, it all takes time—longer than most people imagine . . . you've got to apply those skills and produce goods or services that are valuable to people . . . Grit is about working on something you care about so much that you're willing to stay loyal to it . . . it's doing what you love, but not just falling in love—staying in love." I'm a steadfastly loyal person, perhaps even to a fault. I'll always be loyal to those I love, and I loved my company and all the people it touched. We had paid over

$1 million to women for flexible work at that point and I wanted to keep that going.

Building a start-up comes with moments of feeling beaten down, but those with grit keep standing back up, more determined than before. Grit accumulates over time and has a compound effect. Liz Bohannon, founder and CEO of Sseko Designs, calls this *pluck*. These moments of grit are often private, but it's crucial to remember that others face similar struggles and keep rising, too. During my period of uncertainty about the future of my company, several fellow founders were wrestling with their own challenges. Some had to close their businesses, others managed to arrange acquisitions or sales, and some are still hanging on. Speaking with these women was vital for me during that period. My family and team provided great support, but being the CEO and decision-maker is different, and my friends in similar positions understood exactly what I was going through. I delve more into the importance of having a support system in Chapter 6.

The Ultimate Concern

Well before the acquisition talks started, my journey was sprinkled with stories of grit, each one a stepping stone in the construction of my company. In 2015, after relocating across the country with my young family, I started working as a freelancer while simultaneously being a full-time, stay-at-home mom. It was a daunting balancing act at first, made all the more challenging by the isolation of being a new mother in a strange city. Tears were shed and hardships endured. However, I found solace in a new friendship with a fellow mom, Chloe. Our daughters, born merely months apart, became fast friends, and we followed suit. Our weekly playdates were my sanity lifeline. We both yearned for the flexibility of spending time with our kids while still pursuing a career. Chloe was instrumental in helping me navigate those early years of motherhood and later took on the role of chief operating officer at Allobee. If I could trust her with my kids, I knew I could trust her with my business.

In her book, Duckworth talks about an "ultimate concern," a goal that gives purpose and direction to almost all of your actions. I was beginning to discern what mine was. As I met more moms, I realized that I wasn't alone in my quest for flexible work. This realization became my ultimate concern—promoting flexible work for moms—and it ignited the unyielding grit that would fuel my journey over the next few years.

One day, I received a Facebook message from Kayla, a mom keen on collaborating on a coworking space for parents. She too yearned for flexible work and the camaraderie of a supportive community. We met for coffee one day at the local waffle shop and had a playdate with our girls because they were the same age. We spent hours talking about our dreams and also the need for flexible space and solutions for parents. She shared how she navigated going from being in the restaurant industry to getting a flexible job the day she had her daughter. Kayla can tell this story better than I, but she literally took a call for the job while sitting in the bathroom at the hospital after giving birth because she was that determined to get a flexible job. This is just one example of the grit that Kayla embodies; she is always looking for solutions to make her vision a reality. Together, we envisioned and built what that future might look like—a haven for our community and flexible work for parents. Six months later, we launched The Pod Works, a coworking space for families. The grand opening coincided with my due date for my second child, but fortunately, he decided to hang on for an extra two weeks, giving me enough time to get things off the ground. Collaborators with grit, like Kayla, make excellent partners because they stay true to their ultimate concern. The Pod served as a springboard for dreamers and builders, offering a supportive environment for parents in search of flexible work.

The Pod eventually gained another gritty mom, Natasha, who took over the reins when I decided to shift my focus to building Allobee. The first time I met Natasha, I recognized her as a builder. She identified a need for a Montessori/STEAM (science, technology, engineering, art, and math)-focused school in Tacoma, our city of residence, and took the initiative to establish one. The school had a waitlist even before it opened—moms can recognize a good thing when they see one. I was fortunate enough to get my daughter enrolled, and Natasha became a member of The Pod, too, setting the stage for the future. The Pod now hosts a family of businesses, including a coworking space, a co-lab STEM center, and the Tacoma Children's School.

The idea for Allobee came to me while I was in the nursing room at The Pod. Even in my sleep-deprived state, I couldn't shake off my ultimate concern of advocating for flexible work for moms. I wanted to find a way to fuse my tech skills with my ultimate concern to shape a future where women could thrive. I knew embarking on this new venture wouldn't be easy, but I'm not sure I fully grasped the extent of the challenge at the time.

Initially, Allobee wasn't our chosen name; we started with MOMentum Market. The name served as a reminder that even on tough days, when everything seemed to go awry, I could still take one small step forward, creating momentum. Gradually, these small steps would build substantial momentum and drive us forward. However, we soon realized that there were too many nearby companies using the word *momentum*, and it was affecting us negatively, prompting us to rebrand to Allobee.

The name Allobee also carries significance. *Allo* is derived from *allomothering*, a term that refers to the practice among elephants where the herd collectively cares for a newborn, allowing the mother to recover. This concept resonated with us as we aimed to support our freelancer moms and business owners as they nurtured their "business babies." The *bee* in Allobee speaks to my affinity for bees and their collaborative nature in building a hive, which mirrored our collaborative effort to build something significant. A small victory for all founders out there—securing our domain cost us a mere $8.88!

We launched the company in May 2020. It may seem like an insane time to start a new business, considering the global pandemic and economic recession. Yet, focusing on providing flexible work at a time when everyone was seeking flexibility and remote work options, if possible, seemed to be an ideal solution. Building a start-up amid these challenging circumstances required an enormous amount of grit. However, I believed so deeply in the power of flexible work that I clung to our mission and persisted in building Allobee.

The Dark Side of Grit

Momentum and grit together can be an incredibly potent combination. External forces often provide a nudge, initiating the buildup of momentum, but it's your grit that keeps the wheel spinning even when speed bumps and brick walls stand in your path. The trick is to use your grit to navigate these hurdles, preventing any significant loss of momentum for prolonged periods. As a founder, I felt like I was in constant motion, propelled by the belief that any halt would result in losing the momentum. Although there's some truth to that notion, it led me toward burnout, a side effect I had to learn to manage.

In early summer 2022, burnout had set in. I felt drained and struggled to visualize the path forward, wondering how I would keep going. In hindsight, I wasn't alone—several of my founder friends, many of whom were also moms, were experiencing something similar. We had juggled the responsibilities of raising children and building companies amid a global pandemic, running on fumes for years. However, with so many people depending on us, giving up wasn't an option. Instead, I chose to use my grit differently—I took a pause. I needed a moment to introspect, to reassess what I was fighting for, to refuel, regain momentum, and attain clarity.

The realization that I needed a pause came at a specific moment. One summer day at our farmhouse, without any child-care assistance because I couldn't justify the expense while not drawing a salary from my start-up, I found myself overwhelmed. I was trying to keep overheads low, but the stress culminated in a minor domestic mishap—I burnt the biscuits. When my husband made a comment about the burnt biscuits, something inside me snapped. Overwhelmed, I got into my car and drove to the top of a nearby mountain. I disembarked, walked into a field, and let out a primal scream, releasing years of suppressed frustration. I sat back in my car and wept. Those cows grazing peacefully in the field were in for a surprise, witnessing a millennial mom venting her frustrations. Years of relentless forward motion had left me with no room to breathe.

The darker side of grit is the tendency not to recognize when we need a pause. I am certain that my inability to acknowledge my burnout affected my performance as a founder. I was so engrossed in the process of building that I was oblivious to my own deterioration. I loved what I was building and believed in it deeply, but the strain was taking a toll on me and my loved ones. Eventually, I collected myself, drove home, and apologized to my family. I admitted that I hadn't been managing my feelings well and needed some time. I pledged never to let myself reach that breaking point again. No matter the passion or belief in your venture, it's never worth it if it leads to your or your loved ones' undoing.

Approaches and Tactics for Building Grit and Resilience

Just like building software, building grit is an iterative process that takes time and is strengthened through challenging experiences. It's a muscle you have to work at, akin to debugging complex code, layer by layer, until it's strong and resilient. Here are the strategies that helped me build my grit muscle, much like how a programmer strengthens their coding skills:

- **Grit Tip 1: Cultivate a robust coding ethic:** Growing up in a blue-collar family, I admired the strong work ethic around me, comparable to a coder's unwavering dedication to solving complex problems. The key is to persevere, keep writing your code—work consistently on tasks propelling you toward your goals, even when they're challenging or tedious. This approach has powered me a great distance and continues to fuel my progress.

- **Grit Tip 2: Code with patience:** They say in programming the best code is often written slowly. This principle holds true in life as well—patience is a virtue. It's something I've had to learn, much like mastering a difficult programming language. Success, just like debugging a complex code base, takes time. Recognize that progress can be gradual, but stay committed to your journey. Patience always pays off, perhaps not as expected, but it does.

- **Grit Tip 3: Embrace the agile approach:** In coding, and in life, the ability to adapt is crucial. Just like agile development in software, where iteration is key, adapting to life's curveballs is an important aspect of building grit. Don't hesitate to pivot when needed, and use your creativity to devise new strategies. Keep your ego in check—just like how you wouldn't stick to a faulty code, don't persist in a futile direction.

- **Grit Tip 4: Build resilience into your code:** In coding, errors are a given. They're not roadblocks, but opportunities for improvement. The same goes for life's challenges. Grit equips you with the resilience to rebound from setbacks, much like a well-written code is built to withstand bugs and failures.

- **Grit Tip 5: Prioritize incremental code improvement:** Much like the principle of iterative development in coding, focus on making consistent progress rather than striving for immediate perfection. Celebrate the successful completion of each development sprint in your life. I wish I had taken more time to celebrate the small victories in building Allobee.
- **Grit Tip 6: Practice code self-compassion:** In programming, it's important to be patient with yourself. Likewise, in life, when things don't go as planned, show yourself kindness. Acknowledge your efforts, understand that everyone encounters bugs in their code, or in other words, setbacks in their life's journey. The important part is being kind to yourself throughout the debugging process.

Gritty Women

I trust you've found some inspiration, or perhaps related to, my tales of grit. Now, I'd like to highlight some women whose grit and resilience have inspired me. It's vital to recognize that we are not alone and that others have dug deep to uphold their ultimate values.

Marie Curie: A pioneering scientist, Marie Curie was the first woman to receive a Nobel Prize and remains the only person to have won Nobel Prizes in two different scientific fields—physics and chemistry. Despite facing a slew of challenges and obstacles as a female scientist in a male-dominated field, and enduring the loss of her mother and sister at a tender age, she persevered in her studies. Her tenacity led her to discover the elements polonium and radium, significantly advancing our understanding of radioactivity.

Malala Yousafzai: As a Pakistani advocate for education, Malala Yousafzai became the youngest Nobel Prize laureate at age 17. At 15, the Taliban shot her for advocating for girls' education in Pakistan. Undeterred, after surviving the attack and recovering from her injuries, Malala continued her fight for educational rights. She established the Malala Fund, giving voice to millions of girls globally who are denied education.

Julia Hartz: As cofounder and CEO of Eventbrite, Julia Hartz navigated the male-dominated tech industry to establish a thriving event management and ticketing platform. Despite encountering numerous obstacles and intense competition, Hartz steered Eventbrite into becoming a global company, serving millions of event organizers and attendees.

Whitney Wolfe Herd: The founder and CEO of Bumble, Whitney Wolfe Herd cofounded the dating app Tinder before leaving the company amidst a sexual harassment lawsuit. Turning adversity into motivation, she launched Bumble, a dating app that empowers women by enabling them to make the first move. Today, Bumble is among the most popular dating apps, with more than 100 million users worldwide.

Sara Blakely: As the founder of Spanx, Sara Blakely transformed her concept for comfortable shapewear into a billion-dollar business. She started with merely $5,000 in savings and faced numerous rejections from manufacturers before finding one who believed in her vision. Today, Spanx is a global brand, and Blakely ranks among the world's most successful self-made female entrepreneurs. If you've followed me for a while, you'll know of my slight obsession with Sara; she's one of my favorite businesswomen.

Maya Angelou: A renowned poet, author, and civil rights activist, Maya Angelou surmounted a traumatic childhood and faced numerous adversities throughout her life. Despite these challenges, she became a celebrated writer and a symbol of strength and resilience. Her best-selling autobiography, *I Know Why the Caged Bird Sings*, details her experiences and demonstrates her exceptional spirit and determination. I'll never forget when my grandmother took me to the North Carolina General Assembly to hear Maya speak. I was captivated as she read a poem.

Oprah Winfrey: Born into poverty to a single teenage mother, Oprah Winfrey faced numerous hardships, including abuse and discrimination, in her early life. Despite these challenges, she became one of the world's most influential women, boasting a long-lasting career in media and philanthropy. Her grit and determination have made her an icon and a source of inspiration to millions. I still dream of one day being in the same room as her.

■ ■ ■

These women have become icons in their own right and their stories of grit inspire generations to come. Their success after such determination shows us that we can build the future if we are persistent.

Code Review: Debugging Your Grit

As we close this chapter on grit, let's initiate our first code review. Think of this as a personal debug session for your grit module. Remember, in the coding world, no piece of code is perfect in its first iteration. It's through constant review, tweaking, and debugging that it becomes functional and efficient.

Maybe you're in the early stages of compiling your grit code, or perhaps you're deep in the debugging process already, working tirelessly but feeling like you're grinding your gears. No matter where you are on your journey, initiating a code review can offer a fresh perspective and help optimize your performance.

So, let's dive in and run a code review on your grit module. Reflect on the following debug questions:

- **Debug point:** Recall a time when you faced a significant challenge or setback in your professional life. How did your grit function perform? Were there any bugs you needed to fix to ensure your perseverance?

- **Error log:** How does your grit module respond when it encounters obstacles or difficulties? What updates could help improve its error handling and cultivate more grit in your approach?
- **Success update:** Reflect on a moment when your determination and persistence led to a successful output. What lessons were learned that you could integrate into your grit code base for future reference?
- **Function review:** How does your grit function maintain focus and motivation during execution of difficult tasks or projects? Are there any features you could add to improve its performance?
- **User feedback:** What strategies have you coded into your grit module to help it persevere when it encounters a "program termination" signal (i.e., when you feel like giving up)? Are there any updates or patches needed?
- **Resilience test:** How does your grit code handle exceptions and bounce back from adversity? Are there any algorithms or strategies you could implement to enhance its resilience capabilities?

Think of this code review as a check-in with yourself. It's not just about hunting down what's going wrong, it's also about recognizing what's going right. As you mull over these questions, take a moment to give yourself a pat on the back for all the times your grit module has come into play, helping you push through and persevere. We're all works in progress and the debugging process never really stops. But with each review, you're getting better at understanding yourself and shaping the future you want. Remember, it's about building a better you, one code review at a time, so you can build a better future.

4

Education

Compiling Knowledge, Booting Success

If you don't take the time to think about and analyze your life, you'll never realize all the dots that are all connected.

—Beyoncé

Follow your own lit path, a path of things that excite and light you up; a lit path is one that's fulfilling and dotted with exciting things you're passionate about.

—Miki Agrawal

As I BEGIN this chapter, I find myself reflecting on a journey that's as complex and rewarding as building a software application from scratch. My transition into the tech sector has been nothing short of transformative, with every step rooted in the pursuit of knowledge. I truly believe in the idea that each job, educational moment, and turning point have played their part, shaping me and propelling me forward. Even perceived missteps have contributed to the intricate design of my journey.

In this chapter, I decode my path into distinct phases, akin to the stages in a coding project. Each stage, from self-assessment to

33

the final deployment into my new career, mirrors the process of software development, providing you with an intriguing blueprint for career transition.

Through my personal journey, I share the challenges I faced, the victories I savored, and the resilience it required. As the renowned physicist Albert Einstein once said, "Education is not the learning of facts, but the training of the mind to think," and this is precisely how I leveraged my education—not just to accumulate knowledge but to reimagine my future.

Moreover, I will explore the empowering role of AI tools such as ChatGPT in democratizing tech education and shaping the new-age learning process. As I moved closer to my goal with each challenge met and every line of code understood, I invite you to join me on this exhilarating journey. So, let's dive in, ready to decode my transition into tech, one line at a time.

A New Path Emerges: My Transition into the World of Tech

Having transitioned careers through acquiring more education, I'm a strong advocate for the transformative power of learning. Although some individuals excel at self-teaching and managing their own education, navigating online courses independently was not my strong suit. My husband, a master at self-guided learning, had the ability to do this, but I required a more structured approach. I felt at the time that I needed the legitimacy, the foundational knowledge, and the confidence to break into the technology sector.

I still remember a pivotal night during my graduate school Java class, my first dive into object-oriented programming. Struggling with my code, I sought help from my husband (a computer science major and engineer). He refused, not out of spite, but out of wisdom. I needed to find the solution myself, he insisted, learning from the errors was as crucial as learning to write the code itself. It was a significant lesson, and when I finally got the code to compile, displaying a Tetris-like game on the screen, it was an exhilarating victory. From that moment, I was hooked. My passion for coding was sparked, and I was eager to finish graduate school and apply my newfound skills.

As I progressed through grad school, I found myself drawn to agile project management and product management. Helping to shape a product was a thrill, and I looked forward to doing it professionally in the tech industry or within start-ups. I didn't foresee that one day I'd be building my own tech company. One stark reality that undergraduate and graduate schools did not adequately prepare me for was the challenging job hunt post-graduation. There was an unspoken assumption that graduating was akin to conquering a mountain with job offers waiting at the peak. This was not the reality, at least not for me.

A career transition in your late 20s can be particularly challenging. Despite my years of work experience, I had to accept that I was starting from square one in a new field. This realization was tough, and I found myself applying for roles that, from a hiring manager's perspective, I was not yet qualified for. Recognizing this, I sought opportunities with start-ups that needed my new skills and experience from my past roles. I also embarked on side projects to acquire practical experience that I could list on my résumé.

Looking back, it's like viewing a constellation of experiences, each a star dotting my life's journey. While these dots may seem disconnected up close, from a higher vantage point, they form a beautiful design—a road map to where I am today. Each job, educational moment, and turning point have played their part, shaping me and propelling me forward. Even perceived missteps have contributed to the intricate design of my journey.

I've found a great deal of learning happens on the job, often more than what's gained in a classroom. My nonprofit experience, for instance, honed my public speaking skills, storytelling, fundraising abilities, and an understanding of compliance—vital skills as a founder. Similar to nonprofit work, founding a company requires creativity and resilience, especially when resources are tight.

During my tenure in the nonprofit sector, I began to understand the limitations of my role. Although the hours were long and demanding, just like in start-up culture, there were also restrictions and bureaucracy I didn't have to contend with as an early-stage founder. Despite the long hours and limitations, I found immense value in my time in the nonprofit sector. My experiences there laid a foundation for my later career in tech.

As I've mentioned, after burning out from nonprofit work, I decided to change careers. After a weekend of heightened security threats at the shelter where I was employed, I began contemplating a different career path. I embarked on a journey of introspection and research, continuously led by the thread of desire to do good in the world and assist people. The scope of fulfilling this mission was vast, yet I didn't stumble on the field of technology until a year later. My then-fiancé, now husband, sparked the light bulb moment by showing me a video of the work being carried out at Microsoft, the company he was working for.

As I shared in Chapter 1, that video wasn't just another company presentation; it was a catalyst. It didn't just explain what Microsoft was doing; it painted a vivid picture of the transformative power of technology, giving me a peek into a world where I could merge my desire to do good with an industry that was reshaping the world. This was the moment that tipped me over the edge, driving me to switch my career and venture into the captivating world of tech.

As I reflect on my own career transition, I am often struck by the number of parallels that exist between my journey and the process of coding a new software application. Through numerous interactions and conversations, I've realized that my experience has the potential to serve as a blueprint for others considering a similar path. In the ensuing section, titled "Shaping the Career

Transition Blueprint: Coding a New Path," we'll examine this road map that I inadvertently created, and I will share the steps I took, the choices I made, and the challenges I faced along the way.

From the initial stages of self-reflection and planning, the decision to enroll in a program, and the role of mentorship and guidance, through to the core development phase of gaining hands-on experience, to the final stages of documenting my journey and launching into my new career in tech, each step has its own story and lessons learned. As we journey together through this narrative, my hope is that my experiences may illuminate the path for others considering a similar transition, making the road a little less intimidating and a little more navigable. So let's delve into the intricacies of this journey and unpack the components of this career transition blueprint.

Shaping the Career Transition Blueprint: Coding a New Path

1. **Preparation: Gathering your libraries and modules:** Start with a self-assessment of your skills. Acknowledge that a basic understanding and skills in your desired career are like importing the necessary libraries and modules before you start coding.
2. **The project idea: Selecting your program:** Deciding to go back to school and earn your master's degree was similar to selecting your software project. You reviewed potential programs, compared different schools, and calculated the costs versus benefits. This stage in your career transition is like defining the features of the program you're about to code—it should align with your interests, values, and career objectives.
3. **Initialization: Enrolling in the program:** Choosing to go back to school and being accepted into a program is like initializing your software development project. This step is fundamental—it sets your aspiration into motion.

4. **Mentorship and guidance: Debugging the process:**
   During your program, your professors, classmates, and
   alumni become your "debuggers" and "code reviewers,"
   helping you navigate the complexities of higher education
   and technology. Their input can illuminate hidden issues
   and offer ways to optimize your career transition, akin to a
   collaborative coding project.
5. **Development phase: Coding the application:** The coursework, research projects, and hands-on experience you
   gained during your master's program constitute the "development phase" of your career transition. This is when you
   write and test the code, learn and apply new concepts—
   acquainting yourself with the syntax of your new career.
6. **Documentation and sharing: Committing and pushing
   your updates:** This stage could involve writing a thesis,
   publishing research papers, or sharing your experiences
   and learnings on a blog or social media. By doing this,
   you're committing your updates and pushing them to the
   repository, sharing your journey with others, and building
   your personal brand in the tech space.
7. **Deployment: Transition into tech:** Finally, after complet-
   ing your degree, you transition into your new career. You
   deploy your program, fully prepared and thrilled to start
   your new journey in tech. This moment marks that you
   have successfully completed the development phase and
   are now ready to use the software you've built for its
   intended purpose—your new career in tech.

From Blueprint to Reality: The Final Compilation

Embarking on a career transition is not a decision to be taken
lightly—it's akin to starting a complex coding project, fraught
with challenges and filled with opportunities for learning and
growth. The stages of preparation, choosing the right program,
mentorship, hands-on experience, and finally deploying into a

new career—these are all crucial steps in making a successful transition. As we have seen in my personal journey, each stage required thoughtful reflection, purposeful action, and the right kind of support.

As we transition from this section, it's crucial to remember that although the journey may seem intimidating, the tools, resources, and technology at our disposal today are tremendous aids in this process. One such game-changing tool is AI, specifically, ChatGPT.

AI, like ChatGPT, has made it possible for us to build and create without being expert coders. It has redefined the barriers to entry, bringing about an era when anyone can contribute to technological innovation. I have to admit, I'm a tad envious of the opportunities that today's students and builders have. Having an AI like ChatGPT as a study buddy or a cofounder would have been nothing short of revolutionary during my own transition. I know there is a lot of talk about AI being bad, and, yes, there are major issues that could arise, but the potential to support and augment work right now for humans is pretty powerful. The ability to learn just a small amount of coding can be amplified by the support of AI, helping to accelerate innovation.

In Chapters 8 and 9, we will explore this incredible tool, how it's revolutionizing education and learning, and how it can help you understand, write, and debug code. The days of scrolling endlessly through Stack Overflow are a thing of the past. You can now build a product without being a software engineer. The only requirement is to know just enough to be dangerous. So, keep moving forward with this book as we delve into practical advice on how to leverage these tools and kickstart your journey into the tech world in the upcoming chapters.

Code Review: Education and Transition

In the course of your entrepreneurial journey, your learning and educational experiences will play an instrumental role. They act as the code underlying your knowledge base, the fundamental logic behind your ideas, and the source of inspiration for your innovative approaches. As I've shared throughout this chapter, I've continually relied on my commitment to learning and education as pivotal aspects of my career transitions and growth in the tech industry.

Now, it's time to engage in a code review of your educational experiences. This process is an opportunity to debug and enhance the code that constitutes your learning journey, much like a developer reviews and refines a piece of software code. By reflecting on these questions, you can evaluate how your past experiences have influenced your present attitude toward learning, identify potential areas for improvement, and understand how you can incorporate continuous learning into your future career trajectory.

Remember, this code review isn't a test—rather, it's a method of introspection and self-improvement. I encourage you to take the time to delve into these questions, consider them carefully, and be honest with your responses. As always, the goal here is to enhance your code and improve your overall functionality in the realm of lifelong learning.

- **Review:** How have your past educational experiences shaped your current attitude toward learning?
- **Debug:** Reflect on a time when you felt truly excited about learning something new. What made that experience memorable? Can this excitement code be replicated in future learning experiences?
- **Upgrade:** Think about a skill you've recently learned or a topic you've recently delved into. How has this new knowledge or skill affected your work or personal life?
- **Error handling:** Have you ever faced a significant obstacle or setback in your education or learning journey? How did you overcome it and what did you learn from that experience?

- **Unexplored code:** What is one area or topic that you've always wanted to learn more about but have not yet taken steps to explore? What is holding you back?
- **Code libraries:** Reflect on your most influential mentors, teachers, or guides throughout your life. What qualities did they possess that made their teaching or guidance effective? How can you integrate these libraries into your learning style?
- **Integration:** How do you incorporate continuous learning into your daily routine? What methods or techniques have been effective for you?
- **User interface:** What is your preferred learning style (e.g., auditory, visual, kinesthetic, etc.)? How can you leverage this in your future learning endeavors?
- **Tech stack:** How has the advancement of technology affected your personal learning journey? What digital tools have been most beneficial for your learning?
- **Balance:** How can you better create a balance between formal education and self-directed learning in your life?
- **Innovation:** Reflect on your most innovative learning experiences. Were these experiences driven by traditional methods or did they require thinking outside of the box?
- **Challenge:** In what ways can you challenge the status quo in your current learning strategies to enhance your understanding or skill acquisition?

By the end of this code review, you should have a clearer understanding of your educational code base, including its strengths, areas for improvement, and potential enhancements. Always remember that the process of learning, much like the process of coding, is iterative and continuous. There is always room for improvement, and every experience—every line of code—builds on the previous one. So keep learning, keep coding, and keep growing.

5

Mindset

Reframing the Logic of Your Code

Whether you think you can, or you think you can't—you're right.

—Henry Ford

BUILDING THE FUTURE isn't merely about the physical constructs we see around us or the digital platforms that have become an integral part of our lives. It's also about the intangible edifices we build within ourselves—our mindset. As we continue this journey, let's shift our focus to one of the key building blocks of the GEMS framework: mindset.

Remember how we used LEGO sets to explain the GEMS framework in Chapter 2? Let's revisit that metaphor. Visualize your mindset as a complex LEGO structure, where each brick represents a belief, an experience, a lesson learned. Just as we meticulously construct a LEGO model, we must thoughtfully assemble our mindset to stand robust against doubts and adversities.

As renowned author and businessman Stephen Covey once said, "I am not a product of my circumstances. I am a product of my decisions." In this chapter, we'll delve deep into understanding how our mindset influences our actions, decisions, and ultimately our success.

Imposter syndrome, a phenomenon that plagues many of us, especially women, often acts as a roadblock on our journey to success. Carol S. Dweck, a leading researcher in the field of motivation, said, "Becoming is better than being." We'll explore ways to combat imposter syndrome, reminding ourselves that the journey of growth is ongoing, and that becoming is a constant process that should be embraced.

We'll also discuss the importance of cultivating a future-oriented mindset, equipping ourselves to embrace the challenges and opportunities that come with building for the future.

One particular aspect we'll delve into is coding your mindset: taking cues from the precision, logic, and creativity that goes into computer programming. Similar to programmers shaping complex software from lines of code, we can program our thoughts to foster growth, resilience, and success.

As we embark on this mental engineering journey, let's remember the words of Nelson Mandela, "I never lose. I either win or learn." So, let's roll up our sleeves, flex our mental muscles, and prepare to build a mindset that propels us toward our aspirations, one LEGO brick, or better said, one GEM, at a time.

Banish "I Can't" from Your Vocabulary

Sara Blakely and Jesse Itzler, an entrepreneurial power couple you might recognize from Spanx and Marquis Jet, respectively, have a simple rule in their household: no one is allowed to utter "I can't." With four kids to raise, they understand the deep impact of self-talk and affirmations. In our home, we've adopted this principle, too, and the subtle transformations have been significant. It's startling to realize how frequently "I can't" slips into everyday language from the mouths of my kids and my own. This minor modification to our communication has made a world of difference.

The Runner's Mindset

It's impossible to discuss my mindset without mentioning my journey into running. This was more than just a health kick or a new hobby—it was a commitment to a goal, a promise to push my limits and redefine my self-perception. Throughout my life, I had convinced myself I was terrible at running. But this narrative was self-inflicted and contradicted by my successful stint in track and field during high school and my proficiency in competitive tennis.

Deciding to rewrite my story, I shifted my perspective. After seeing how my mindset had shaped my career trajectory and accomplishments in building companies, I knew I needed to tackle the limitations I had imposed on my physical abilities. I set out on a mission to change my narrative, not only for myself but for my kids. I wanted to be an "active" mom and keep pace with my kids on our hikes, not lagging behind.

From Hiking to Running

Our hiking frequency improved to once a week, and even more in the summer, as I achieved my goal of becoming more active. But, as someone who is naturally ambitious, I sought a new challenge. The desire to run a marathon was born out of a need to alter my mindset in a non-career-related area. Only 1% of people complete marathons, and it appealed to my love for being part of a select group of achievers (https://marathonhandbook.com/how-many-people-have-run-a-marathon/).

But, I knew better than to jump straight into a half-marathon. Instead, I signed up for an 8K race that would earn me a medal—a cowbell that my son had his eyes on. I delayed training due to fear of failure, but when I finally began four weeks before the race, my resolve was stronger than ever. Despite my under-preparation, the mantras I kept repeating, and the promise I had made to my son, helped me cross the finish line. The overwhelming emotions at the end of the race were a clear testament that the stories I had been telling myself about my athletic capabilities were indeed self-created limitations.

Running to Inspire

That first race sparked an enthusiasm for running in me. But, life happened, my routine fell apart, and my next race wasn't until the fall. In the midst of this lull, I turned to the inspirational stories of other runners. I closely followed the Western States Endurance Run, a 100-mile race, which saw the triumph of ultra-runner Courtney Dauwalter and the unfortunate exit of Callie Vinson, a runner I had just started following.

These two contrasting outcomes—Callie's heartbreak and Courtney's record-breaking performance—epitomized the very essence of running for me. Running is life lived at a different pace, a series of peaks and valleys that we navigate one step at a time. Whether it's a smooth ride or a rocky trail, the race, like life, owes us nothing. It's our responsibility to show up, give our best, and learn from the experience. As entrepreneur Jesse Itzler puts it, we need to "empty our tank," give everything we have, irrespective of the outcome. By doing so, we validate our place in the race and in life.

In Chapter 6, I'll share more on how a robust support system was crucial to my running journey and how, whether you're a novice or getting back into running, you should never underestimate the power of support.

Imposter Syndrome, Yep That Again

We often do not feel that we belong in the rooms that we enter. Almost every organization with women in it has talks and conversations about imposter syndrome. I rarely see men talking about it. My theory is that women have always felt we had to prove ourselves in every room or situation we are in. We sometimes are the only woman in the room and that can easily bring on imposter syndrome. Yet, I have found that women see even more imposter syndrome in other rooms of women. We compare ourselves and hold ourselves to such insane standards that we have a hard time feeling like we belong or are worthy. The amount of energy we spend on this hurts us as women.

When I was speaking on stage at the Bull City Summit in Durham, North Carolina, in 2022, I was asked by an audience member how I handled imposter syndrome. I was a little feisty that day and frustrated after a summer of trying to fundraise and not meeting my goal. So I said, "Would you have asked me that if I was a man?" and I definitely took her and the audience off guard, but she responded with, "Wow, you are right, I probably would not have." I knew why she asked, and I was glad to respond and share my tips and stories of my own battle with imposter syndrome because I know as women we need to see that others have overcome it or are at least getting past it quicker when it arises. I will share some of the stories and strategies of imposter syndrome in the next sections.

I tend to jump into new things head first and get to work. This has helped me not dwell as much on imposter syndrome because I am already doing the work before the imposter syndrome starts to creep in. This provides me with some perspective because I know I am already capable of starting or being in the same room. I very much felt this in grad school because I jumped right in, got accepted, and started classes. I remember feeling a little imposter syndrome creep in when I started meeting my classmates and hearing their backgrounds but I put in the work, worked harder when I struggled, and I got to the finish line.

I had been stalking a group called All Day Running Company for months and one of their founders, Jesse Itzler, is Sara Blakely's (founder of Spanx) husband. They announced a festival called

Runningman, kind of like Burning Man but for runners, and even before the announcement, I just knew it was something I needed to do; my gut was yelling at me to sign up. Yet the pricing was rather high, my running friend could not come on those dates, and we were coming off five months of my husband not having a job, so logically it was not a good choice. There was also a factor in there of imposter syndrome. I had just started running; was I even really a runner yet? What was I thinking, going to a *running* event, leaving my family for three days in the middle of the fall to go to a festival? This was going to not just be about running, though; there were speakers and it was going to be about up-leveling. What I have learned about mindset through the years is that, just like grit, it is a muscle you have to keep working and pushing on or it will not expand and grow. Through my coaching experience for the last six months, I realized that I needed more experiences of community in my life that had nothing to do with my career. Places to find people that might intersect with who I had become and where I am going. Jesse talks a lot about how his friends have changed through the years as he has changed, but he always makes family and friends a huge part of his life. Coming off building for years and heads down with that and family, I got to the other side and realized I left behind a lot of friendships or they just did not fit with where I was now.

As women we are pulled in so many different directions, so many buckets we have to fill for others that there is such little time at the end of the day to fill our own. I knew that I needed to fill my bucket or I would burn out again. I made a deal with myself. If a $3K engagement came in from speaking or consulting, and I finished the 8K race under the time limit, then I would sign up for the festival. The $3K project landed. That meant it was time to say yes to Runningman. It is not hard to press a button and pay for a festival, but it would be hard getting past imposter syndrome leading up to the event. That is where my tried-and-true strategies would come in. Some of the following strategies might sound crazy, but I promise you they work. And I think when it comes to imposter syndrome, we have to almost get out of our body and mind for a moment and do something almost silly to get out of our heads.

Embrace Your Inner Blowfish

Remember the TV show *Breaking Bad*, where a high school teacher transforms into a meth dealer? There's a particular scene in which Walt, the teacher, attempts to embolden his partner, Jesse, by telling him that he's a blowfish. Jesse can puff himself up, make himself seem bigger and more formidable when necessary. I've adopted this metaphor before every significant speaking engagement or crucial meeting I attend. For that moment, I am a blowfish, inflated to my full capacity, embodying the best version of myself, ready to dominate the stage. As an ambivert, the thought of maintaining this blowfish state for extended periods can be daunting. Yet, knowing that I can deflate afterward empowers me to pour all my energy into owning the moment. So, the next time imposter syndrome strikes, puff yourself up, embrace your blowfish energy, and own the room!

Embody the Confidence of a Stanford Grad

During my relentless pitching for start-up funding, I reached out to numerous individuals, seeking advice on delivering effective pitches. One memorable piece of advice suggested that I channel the confidence of a white male Stanford graduate sporting a hoodie. Initially, I laughed it off, but on reflection, the advice struck a chord. With less than 2% of funding going to women, often due to biases and pattern recognition, why not try a different approach (https://techcrunch.com/2023/01/18/women-founded-startups-raised-1–9-of-all-vc-funds-in-2022-a-drop-from-2021/)? Why not enter these spaces with an air of male confidence? So, in 2020 and

2021, before zooming into investor calls, I psyched myself up, visualizing how tech titans like Mark Zuckerberg would handle these interactions. Remember, if you need to ace an investor call and shake off imposter syndrome, consider harnessing that male energy. Take a leaf out of their book, channel their confidence, and go conquer the world.

Embrace the Process: You've Earned Your Place

Imposter syndrome can often be rooted in a belief that you lack the necessary knowledge or expertise. But here's a secret weapon against that: the power of preparation. When you invest time in continuous learning, you equip yourself with a wealth of information that can boost your confidence and help you project an aura of expertise. Remember, there's no shortcut to proficiency; you have to put in the work, show up daily, and push yourself to achieve more.

Consider my experience with running. I can't just show up at a race without prior training and expect to excel. If I do, I'd inevitably struggle to reach the finish line, and that's when imposter syndrome would swoop in, uninvited. But if I rigorously train; educate myself about running; focus on recovery, strength training, and cross-training; nourish my body correctly; and then approach the race, I can be confident in my preparedness.

So, the key is not just hard work but also crafting a mantra that resonates with your journey and preparedness. This mantra can be your mental armor against creeping imposter syndrome. During my first race, I found myself doubting my abilities at mile 3, wondering, "What on earth were you thinking? You're not a runner!" But then I recalled my mantra: "You have trained for this." I repeated it like a chant as I tackled the uphill struggle of mile 3, and it worked. The last mile felt empowering because I knew I was well prepared and fully deserved to be there. Your mindset is your strongest ally—remind yourself that you've earned your place.

Cultivating a Layered Mindset

Establishing an overall positive mindset is essential, but it's just the tip of the iceberg. Mindset, in my experience, operates in layers. Although an overarching positive outlook is crucial, it's equally important to develop more nuanced mindsets that cater to different aspects of life. I've found that nurturing both a business mindset and a personal mindset serves me well, and these two mentalities often bolster each other. Again, it comes down to putting in the work and being ready to tap into the appropriate mindset when faced with challenges in your professional or personal life.

Take the case of Jesse Itzler, whom I recently heard on a podcast speaking about training for a 100-mile race. He found himself hitting a mental roadblock at 35 miles. Enter Chad Wright, a former Navy SEAL, who worked with Jesse solely on mindset techniques. Jesse hit a wall and was even hypothermic during the race, but Chad introduced him to a miraculous mindset: "I don't get tired." Despite initial resistance, Jesse began repeating it, and to his surprise, he made it to the 100-mile mark. This tenacity is precisely the type of mindset I strive for in my personal pursuits like running. Although it could apply to business as well, I find that a different approach is required there.

When it comes to cultivating my entrepreneurial mindset, I draw inspiration from Brian Tracy's book, *Eat That Frog*, which I read when I first started delving into personal development books over a decade ago. At the time, I was battling procrastination on my goals, but Tracy's simple principles transformed my outlook and enabled me to stop deferring my objectives. I learned how to navigate setbacks and potential failures without getting stuck in the vortex of negative emotions. I give myself a set time to feel the disappointment, but once that time elapses, it's time to move on.

Tracy's advice on constantly verbalizing your goals has also been invaluable. Speaking out loud about your aspirations lends them substance and, when shared with others, introduces an element of accountability. These principles have been integral to my success as an entrepreneur and in achieving my personal goals.

Believing in our individual capacity to change the world is the first step toward making it happen. It may not always make the news, but every personal transformation can create a ripple effect, leading to broader societal changes. Each one of us, in our unique ways, contributes to shaping the future.

Coding Your Entrepreneurial Mindset: A Developer's Guide to Success

I've often likened the process of cultivating this mindset to coding: it involves the right commands, syntax, and logic. Just as in programming, each one of us can code our mindset to optimize our entrepreneurial journey. Therefore, I present to you a developer's guide to success, a manual to help you understand how to cultivate an entrepreneurial mindset. The journey to entrepreneurial success starts within, rooted in self-awareness, resilience, and ambition. Here are some strategies tailored specifically to foster this entrepreneurial perspective:

1. **Debugging over perfection:** Adopt the debugging mindset, understanding that your skills and knowledge base will evolve over time. As an entrepreneur, you won't have the complete code base from the start. Embrace the journey of learning and acknowledge that bugs and errors are opportunities for enhancement, not setbacks.

2. **Error handling and recovery:** In entrepreneurship, just like in programming, errors are stepping stones to success. They provide crucial lessons that help refine business logic. Treat errors as occasions to refactor and improve your code, rather than fatal system crashes.

3. **Positive commenting:** Practice constructive self-dialogue, akin to leaving helpful comments in your code. Replace

thoughts such as "This bug is too complex" with "I can resolve this bug one line of code at a time." This positive self-talk can elevate your confidence, motivation, and persistence—all vital in entrepreneurship.

4. **Breaking down your functions:** Define what success means in your entrepreneurial journey. Segment your overarching goals into smaller, manageable functions or modules. This clarity and structure can drive your daily operations and keep you motivated when dealing with complex code bases or business challenges.

5. **Code visualization:** Regularly envision your code running flawlessly, achieving the desired output. Visualization is a powerful tool that can increase your motivation and make your entrepreneurial dreams feel more attainable.

6. **Appreciating your commitments:** Take time to acknowledge and appreciate your incremental achievements, however small. Celebrating every successful commitment not only improves your mood but also fosters a positive and proactive attitude—essential for tackling entrepreneurial challenges.

7. **Mindful coding and meditation:** Incorporate mindfulness practices into your coding routine. Focusing on the present line of code can reduce stress, boost creativity, and improve problem-solving skills—all essential for entrepreneurial success.

8. **Code reviews and networking:** Interact with other developers and entrepreneurs. They can provide valuable insights, feedback, and support. Remember, entrepreneurship—like coding—doesn't have to be a solitary journey.

9. **Embracing continuous learning:** The tech and business world is constantly evolving. Regularly updating your knowledge and learning new languages or frameworks not only keeps you competitive but also fuels innovation and growth.

10. **Balancing work and rest:** Prioritizing your physical well-being is integral to maintaining a healthy coding and entrepreneurial mindset. Regular breaks from the screen, balanced nutrition, and adequate rest can significantly influence your energy levels, decision-making skills, and overall performance.

Achieving success truly starts within your text editor. Cultivating an entrepreneurial mindset involves recognizing your internal strengths, committing to growth, and understanding that the journey of entrepreneurship—like coding—is as valuable as the destination.

Unleash Your Intrapreneurial Spirit: Building a Brighter Future from Within Your 9-to-5

In this journey of building a brighter future, not every woman envisions herself leaving her 9-to-5 job to start her own company. Some find their passion, purpose, and fulfillment within the structure of an existing organization, and that's perfectly okay. I want you to know that you too can be a trailblazer, an innovator, and a leader within the familiar confines of your workplace. You can be an intrapreneur.

What Is an Intrapreneur?

An intrapreneur is an employee who applies the principles of entrepreneurship within a larger organization to drive innovation, create new opportunities, and contribute to the company's growth. Think of it as being a start-up founder, but within the safety net of an established corporation.

The Power of Intrapreneurship

Being an intrapreneur comes with several advantages:

- **Resources at your fingertips:** You have access to the resources, infrastructure, and funding of a larger organization, which can significantly accelerate your projects.

- **Reduced risk:** Unlike entrepreneurs who take on personal financial risk, intrapreneurs operate within the security of a salaried position.
- **Influence and impact:** Intrapreneurs often have a direct line to decision-makers, making it easier to champion and implement innovative ideas.
- **Learning ground:** It's a fantastic opportunity to learn, experiment, and grow without the pressures and risks associated with starting your own venture.

I've always struggled working at a traditional job because I wanted to have an impact and build, but I didn't know how to do that within the confines of a 9-to-5 role. I bet many of you can relate to this feeling of wanting more.

My journey led me to a pivotal book titled *Impact Players: How to Take the Lead, Play Bigger, and Multiply Your Impact* by Liz Wiseman, a renowned consultant who has worked with some of Silicon Valley's biggest companies. Wiseman's book emphasizes how impact players seek out the real job that needs to be done, strive to improve processes, and support the overall vision of their company and team.

I believe that with the right support, these impact players could also be great at innovating within the company because they are looking for areas that can be changed that others are not looking for. My experiences echo the notion that intrapreneurs have the potential to drive innovation, even within well-established organizations.

The SAS Example: Supporting Intrapreneurship

Companies like SAS, headquartered in North Carolina, are notable for their support of employees' outside endeavors. Here, employees have launched diverse ventures, from bakeries to legal practices supporting start-ups. This approach enables employees to nurture their creative and entrepreneurial spirits while simultaneously contributing to the company's success.

This kind of support fosters a sense of ownership, engagement, and entrepreneurial drive among employees, ultimately enhancing retention.

The Broader Relevance: Technology Skills for All

The demand for technical skills isn't limited to start-ups. Every company today needs some form of technology expertise. The more technology skills you can bring to the table, the better positioned you are for success, whether you decide to pioneer your venture or spearhead innovation within your organization.

The knowledge you gain from this book, especially from Chapters 8 and 9, can be immensely beneficial. These chapters delve into essential aspects of entrepreneurship, innovation, and the practical use of technology. They equip you with the skills to identify areas ripe for change and the tools to transform ideas into reality.

Intrapreneurship offers a dynamic pathway for women who wish to make a significant impact, build a brighter future, and harness the full extent of their technical knowledge, all while thriving within the structure of their 9-to-5 careers. So, embrace your potential as an intrapreneur, lead innovation, and let your journey of building a better tomorrow begin right where you are.

Code Review: Debugging Your Mindset

Now that we've examined the foundational building blocks of a strong entrepreneurial mindset, let's shift our focus to something every developer and entrepreneur alike understands: the importance of constant review, reflection, and optimization. Just as software developers use code reviews to assess and improve their work, we need to scrutinize our mindsets with the same level of critical evaluation.

It's not enough to merely build our mindsets; we must regularly debug them, identify any weak spots or misalignments, and make necessary adjustments to optimize our mindset for success. This process isn't always easy—it requires honesty, openness, and a willingness to confront our preconceptions and biases. But it's also an opportunity for growth and transformation.

With that said, it's time to enter our code review phase, specifically crafted to help you debug your mindset. This debugging process isn't about finding faults in your thinking, but rather identifying areas for enhancement and fine-tuning your mindset to support your entrepreneurial journey better. It's a check-in, an opportunity to reflect, reassess, and recalibrate. Your mindset, much like a piece of code, underpins how you operate. It's vital to ensure it's optimized for success. Here's a set of review questions for you to reflect on:

- **Debugging growth over perfection:** Think about a time when you focused on growth rather than perfection. How did this affect your approach to a task or project? Consider how this mindset could benefit you moving forward.
- **Analyzing and reframing failure:** Reflect on a failure you've experienced in your professional or personal life. How did you handle it at the time? How could you reframe this failure as a stepping stone toward success?
- **Evaluating positive affirmations:** Do you use positive affirmations regularly? If so, how have they affected your confidence and motivation? If not, consider some affirmations you might adopt to boost your entrepreneurial mindset.
- **Inspecting goal-setting mechanisms:** How do you currently set goals? Are they clear and actionable? How could you improve your goal setting to make them more achievable and aligned with your entrepreneurial aspirations?
- **Decoding visualization techniques:** Have you tried visualizing your success? If so, how has this affected your

motivation and confidence? If not, consider how you could incorporate visualization into your daily routine.

- **Debugging gratitude practices:** Do you make time to acknowledge your achievements and express gratitude? How could this practice improve your mood and perspective?
- **Reviewing mindfulness and meditation:** Do you practice mindfulness or meditation? How has it influenced your stress levels and creativity? If not, think about how you might incorporate these practices into your routine.
- **Evaluating networking and mentorship:** Consider your network. Are there entrepreneurs or mentors you could connect with for advice and support? If you're already connected, how have these relationships influenced your entrepreneurial journey?
- **Inspecting commitment to lifelong learning:** How committed are you to lifelong learning? Are there areas of your knowledge that you could update or expand?
- **Debugging self-care practices:** How do you prioritize self-care? How does this affect your energy levels, decision-making skills, and overall performance?

Debugging your mindset enables you to assess and recalibrate your approach. The insights gained will equip you with a stronger, more resilient entrepreneurial mindset, ready for the challenges and triumphs of your journey. Remember to commit to your changes after debugging—action is key. Reflect on your insights, but also decide how you will implement the changes to reinforce a growth mindset.

6

Support

Strengthening the Foundation of Your Code

We all need someone who inspires us to do better than we know how.
—Carol Ann Tomlinson

WE OFTEN TALK about the power of networks, the strength of the tribe, and the impact of community in the entrepreneurial journey. Indeed, these facets of support are crucial for anyone navigating the complex waters of business, particularly for women entrepreneurs who are carving their own paths. But the concept of support goes beyond professional circles; it permeates every aspect of our lives. It's seen in our relationships, our families, and even in our interactions with ourselves. This support is a dual pathway—we receive it, but we also give it.

In this chapter, I want to dive into the fundamental role of support in women's entrepreneurial journeys and, more broadly, in their lives. I will share some of my own experiences and insights, as well as those of remarkable women I've had the privilege of connecting with. The stories and strategies outlined here aim to highlight the transformative power of support, and to encourage us all to foster a culture of collaboration, mentorship, and mutual aid.

From my own narrative as a founder and mother to the inspiring dialogue with Hitha Palepu, we will explore the many forms of support that fuel our aspirations. We will delve into the cruciality of nurturing our networks, guided by the wisdom of Molly Beck's book *Reach Out*. And finally, through a coding-inspired framework, we will examine how to build and maintain a robust, supportive network.

So, let's embark on this journey of discovery, learning, and reflection to understand the intricate tapestry of support that underpins our successes and powers our futures.

What I Told Duke MBA Students

During an event at Duke University, where I was invited to address the MBA students, I found myself in a pre-event conversation with one of the student leaders. She posed an intriguing question to me: "As an entrepreneur, what advice would you offer us?" My answer was instinctive, shaped by the countless experiences and challenges I've faced throughout my entrepreneurial journey: "Above all else, construct a robust network of support."

In my experience, support is the vital, yet often overlooked, ingredient in the recipe for entrepreneurial success. This support can be as diverse as the challenges an entrepreneur faces. It may manifest as a business network that opens doors to opportunities, or as a personal support system that provides resilience in the face of adversity. Both are indispensable if you aspire to shape the future.

This chapter aims to illuminate the role that support has played in my own journey—often appearing in unexpected forms and at unforeseen junctures. More important, I hope to provide you with practical strategies to cultivate the support network you need to navigate your own path. Whether it's advice from a mentor, encouragement from a loved one, or a connection that leads to your next big opportunity, each form of support contributes to your growth and resilience as an entrepreneur.

Running into Support

In Chapter 5, you learned about my transformation into a runner and the enormous support that made it possible. This support appeared in diverse forms—from running communities and books to my family, and notably, my friend, Kesa.

I publicly declared my intent to run a half marathon before I turned 40 at the end of 2022. By broadcasting my goal to the universe and my network, I hoped to be held accountable. Kesa, who'd embarked on her own running journey at the insistence of her 5K-running son, reached out. I knew she hadn't been a runner before and didn't even like running initially, so I felt she truly understood my struggles.

Despite my well-meaning intentions, my personal health and wellness goals often took a backseat to my career ambitions. I've always found it challenging to allot time and energy to personal goals while engrossed in building a company. With the sale of my company, I knew it was time for a shift. I needed to channel my energy elsewhere, and running was my chosen conduit.

However, the beginning was difficult. I started with walking and felt great about it. But the thought of transitioning to running filled me with imposter syndrome. Despite my apprehensions, Kesa persisted, sending me running memes and resources. About five weeks before my planned race, I laced up my shoes and stepped out for my first run.

It wasn't a scene of elegance, but I survived. Kesa, connected to me via Apple Watch, cheered me on after each run. I couldn't help but keep showing up. I had to earn that medal for my son, and now, others knew it, too. To prevent any chance of backing out, I shared my upcoming race on social media. Unlike my previous race attempt, I refused to let fear deter me.

On June 3, Kesa and I both ran our races. Even though we were 900 miles apart, together we completed our challenging tasks and held each other accountable. We're now planning to run a half marathon together. Through this experience, I've realized that running, similar to many endeavors in life, is about mindset and support.

Female Founder Support

Entering the world of female founders is truly an exciting adventure. I distinctly remember my initial encounter with this inspiring community at a Female Founder Alliance event in Seattle. The gathering showcased the diverse range of companies that had thrived under their guidance. I had the opportunity to journey from Tacoma to Seattle with another trailblazing female founder, Laura Malcolm, the founder and CEO of Give InKind.

Give InKind is a pioneering social platform designed to offer support and build connections during times of crisis or need. Laura, a mom and mission-driven founder, was at that time passionately developing her start-up. She has since achieved a successful exit, but not before significantly shaping her company. I am grateful to Laura for inviting me to join her for this event, providing me with a valuable glimpse into the dynamic world I was stepping into.

Back in the early stages of my founder journey, the path forward was filled with uncertainty. However, being in the presence of other women, many of whom were also mothers with young children, who were fervently building impactful companies, was deeply inspiring. It was heartening to see that I wasn't alone in the arena. Many were there with me, each dedicatedly working toward building a better future in their distinctive ways.

Partner Support: Get Yourself an Edgar

I've engaged in countless conversations with women entrepreneurs who shared stories of their partners—stories that warmed my heart or made my stomach turn. Being a partner to an entrepreneur is a tremendous undertaking; I can only imagine the ripples that my entrepreneurial journey has created in my own family life. Yet, through the ebbs and flows of establishing a company, nurturing two young children, weathering a pandemic, and more—all without the support of nearby family—I never doubted the resilience of my relationship with my husband, Edgar.

Each rocky life event has solidified our bond, fortifying our partnership against whatever life throws our way. To some, it may sound cliché, but Edgar is truly my best friend and soulmate. He has an uncanny ability to read my emotional state, stepping in with calming words and reassuring embraces when I start to spiral. He believed in the power of my ideas even before I fully grasped their potential. He was not just my personal cheerleader but also Allobee's, providing advice on business security, brainstorming product ideas, and offering a fresh perspective on engineering issues. Never once did he consider my job as less than his, even during those challenging early stages when I wasn't drawing a salary.

Edgar's support for my goals was not limited to his faith in me; it manifested in tangible actions that made my dreams possible. This became especially apparent during a summer when we found ourselves tucked away in our mountain farmhouse in Sparta, North Carolina. Usually, this was our time to unwind, but I found myself wrestling with the formidable challenge of writing this book, and without any childcare to ease the load.

As both Edgar and I grappled with personal ambitions, he suggested a novel idea—waking up at 4:30 a.m. every day. We had attempted rising at 5 a.m. before, but it proved unfeasible. Now, Edgar introduced me to the spiritual significance of the hour of 4:30 a.m., rooted in a concept called Brahmamuhurtha. This term refers to a 48-minute span that begins one hour and 36 minutes before sunrise and ends 48 minutes before sunrise. Edgar explained that this period is considered auspicious for all forms of yoga and is especially suitable for meditation, worship, or any other spiritual practice. Activities of a spiritual nature undertaken during this time purportedly exert a greater impact than those performed at any other time of the day.

For me, writing has always been akin to a spiritual practice, so I was intrigued and willing to try this idea—I was, in truth, quite desperate. Despite the potential difficulties of shifting our habitual late-night summer routines, Edgar reassured me that we would face the challenge of the early morning together.

A few weeks into this novel routine, we found it to be surprisingly effective! We were both making headway on our early morning goals, and I was finally transcribing my thoughts onto these pages. Taking a leaf out of Brian Tracy's book, *Eat That Frog!* Edgar and I had successfully risen to the challenge, beginning our days by tackling our most daunting tasks—and succeeding.

This immense support from Edgar proved invaluable as I constructed my future. I will forever be grateful not only for Edgar allowing me to build but also actively helping me do so. So, as I often tell people, find yourself an Edgar, or at least acknowledge that the geeky guys are truly the best.

The Power of Support, an Interview with Hitha Palepu

Support plays a vital role in building a future for women, and it comes not only from professional networks but also from friends, family, and the home environment. During my conversations for this book, I had the opportunity to interview Hitha Palepu, a friend and fellow multi-hyphenate entrepreneur. Hitha is an author, CEO of Rhoshan Pharmaceuticals, creator, speaker, wife, and mother of two boys. Here's what she shared:

I want to discuss the importance of support, especially as someone with privilege. What my teams look like, both at home and outside, is a testament to the fact that I can't do it all alone. I owe much of my success to the incredible support system I have. It started with my amazing parents, whom I still cherish spending time with. I was also fortunate to have extended family members, like aunts and grandmothers, who would stay with us for months and take care of me. Additionally, there were close family friends who shared the load of child-rearing and played a significant role in my upbringing. To this day, I maintain a deep bond with them.

My mom, in particular, showed me from an early age that building a village is necessary. She defied the notion of the nuclear family and exemplified the importance of teamwork. This mindset carried into my teenage years, whe[n] I joined numerous clubs and led teams. For instance, running the school newspaper in my senior year provided me with valuable experience in building and leading a team. The concept of building a team continued throughout college and beyond.

When I became a mother, I was fortunate to have my parents relocate to New York for a period of time. Eventually, we decided to create a multi-generational home together. This arrangement allowed my parents to spend as much time with us as they wanted while giving us all our own space. My mom even helped me hire a nanny because I was clueless as a new mom. I relied on her guidance not only for childcare but also for managing our home team. We had a housekeeper who had been with us for four years, and when she expressed her desire to pursue other opportunities, we fully supported her transition to running an in-home childcare system. Supporting our team members' dreams is crucial, and I consistently check in with both my work and home teams to provide assistance and guidance.

My ability to do what I do is heavily reliant on support in various ways. In a world struggling with a loneliness epidemic, we need to shatter the myth of rugged individualism and embrace the power of collaboration. It's essential to share and be transparent about the support we receive on our journey. I am far from being self-made, and I am passionate about rewriting that narrative. By being open about my privilege and accomplishments, I hope to normalize the idea and inspire others who have similar resources to do the same. It also helps alleviate the pressure on those who feel they must do everything alone. Transparency levels the playing field mentally, and it's the right thing to do for your team. I'm immensely grateful for the support I have, as it enables me to pursue my goals.

This excerpt from my interview with Hitha Palepu sheds light on the pivotal role support plays in the lives of women. It highlights the importance of building a strong network and being transparent about the assistance we receive. By recognizing and appreciating the support we have, we can create a more inclusive and empowering future for women.

Building and Nurturing Your Support Network: A Path to Success

As you have seen in my stories, having a strong network is the cornerstone of success in today's interconnected world. It is the catalyst that propels us forward, opens doors to new opportunities, and provides the support we need to navigate challenges. Over the past several years, I have personally experienced the transformative impact of networking and witnessed the remarkable rewards that come from it. And one resource that has been instrumental in my networking journey is the book *Reach Out* by Molly Beck.

Reach Out has been a game-changer for me. Its simplistic yet actionable approach enabled me to build and maintain a network that has consistently delivered outstanding results. This book offers practical strategies that are easy to implement and follow through on, ensuring that networking becomes a seamless part of our lives.

What sets *Reach Out* apart is its emphasis on practicality. Molly Beck breaks down the process of networking into simple steps, making it accessible to everyone, regardless of their background or experience. The book guides readers in identifying potential contacts, leveraging social media platforms, attending networking events, and conducting informational interviews. Molly Beck's insights and advice empower readers to take control of their networking journeys.

Implementing the strategies outlined in *Reach Out* has been a transformative experience. I have seen firsthand the power of reaching out and fostering genuine connections. By following the book's guidance, I have been able to establish a support network of professionals, mentors, and like-minded individuals who have been instrumental in my personal and professional growth.

In this section, inspired by the practical wisdom of *Reach Out*, we delve into the key principles of networking and explore how to build, maintain, and nurture a supportive network. Drawing from my own experiences and insights gained from Molly Beck's book, we uncover effective strategies for building lasting connections and reaping the rewards of a robust network.

Join me as we embark on this journey of harnessing the power of networking. Together, we will discover how these actionable strategies can help us build meaningful relationships, unlock new opportunities, and pave the way for a successful and fulfilling future.

Building Your Network: Writing Your Support Code

As I've journeyed through the multifaceted landscape of entrepreneurship, I've come to understand the value of a robust network and support system. My successes, although my own, have been significantly influenced by the support of mentors, peers, and even rivals who have offered wisdom, guidance, and at times, much-needed reality checks. I am the entrepreneur I am today because of the strong network I've cultivated over the years.

Drawing from these experiences, I wanted to offer you actionable tips and strategies to establish and nurture your own support network. Much like a well-written code is essential for the functioning of a software program, a solid support network can be the linchpin for your success. With this in mind, I present to you a coding-inspired approach to building your network and fostering supportive relationships.

The aim here is to take the learnings from my stories and transform them into practical, actionable steps that can be used to code your own network of support. Let's break down this process, borrowing terminology from the world of coding, to make it relatable, fun, and, most important, effective.

Remember, you're not writing this code in isolation. Your network—your team of key coders—is here to help. So, let's dive into the code of support, debugging any issues and iterating along the way. After all, you're the architect of your network, and it's time to start coding.

Constructing Your Support Framework: Identifying and Engaging with Key Coders

- **Identify the key coders:** Start by identifying the people in your network who can assist you in your career transition. These could be colleagues, mentors, or professionals you've met at conferences, much like identifying key coders who contribute significantly to a software project.

- **Social media platforms: The source code repositories:** Consider platforms like LinkedIn as your source code repositories, where you can find potential connections, join relevant groups, and engage in discussions to better understand your industry.
- **Networking events: The code sprints:** Attend industry events like you would participate in code sprints, focused sessions where you meet like-minded professionals to collaborate and share insights with.
- **Informational interviews: The code reviews:** Reach out to professionals in your desired field for informational interviews. These sessions can be seen as code reviews, where you learn more about the field and build meaningful connections.

Maintaining a Supportive Network: Updating Your Support Code

- **Regular communication: The incremental updates:** Maintain your connections by sharing interesting articles, checking in, and maintaining meaningful conversations, similar to incremental updates that keep your code base relevant and responsive.
- **Express gratitude: The acknowledgments in code documentation:** Show appreciation for the support you receive by expressing gratitude, much like acknowledging contributors in your code documentation.
- **Reciprocity: The code refactoring:** Seek opportunities to support your contacts, just as you would refactor your code to improve its structure and design. This could be through sharing job postings, making introductions, or offering your expertise.
- **Keep your network updated: The version control:** Regularly update your network on your career progress, akin to maintaining version control in your code base, ensuring your progress is visible and acknowledged.

Establishing and Cultivating Support Systems: Writing Your Support Functions

- **Define your needs: The function specifications:** Identify the specific type of support you need, such as emotional support, guidance, or professional advice. This is akin to clearly defining the specifications for a function in your code.
- **Identify key individuals: The core functions:** Identify the people in your network who can provide the support you need. They form the core functions in your support code.
- **Maintain regular contact: The regular function calls:** Regularly communicate with your support system, sharing experiences and seeking guidance, much like making regular function calls in your code.
- **Reciprocal support: The extensions and libraries:** Be ready to assist when your contacts need support, just like extending your code or using libraries to enhance its functionality.

Remember, building a network and support system is much like writing and maintaining your code: it requires clarity, collaboration, regular updates, and reciprocity. Authenticity, showing genuine interest, and giving as much as you receive are key principles that will help you establish a robust support code for your success.

Code Review—Debugging Your Support Network

As we wrap up our discussion on our GEMS element, support, it's time for another code review. We are going to debug our support module today. In programming, it's often the case that we cannot do it all alone. We rely on a community of coders who have faced similar bugs, who can offer solutions and shortcuts that have been tested and tried. This communal support is analogous to the network of mentors, allies, and friends who are essential to your success journey.

Just like you wouldn't want to have bugs in your code, gaps in your support network can be equally detrimental. Therefore, it's vital to regularly review your support code and make necessary adjustments. Let's debug together with the following code review questions:

- **Dependencies:** Who are the key individuals or dependencies in your support network? How have they contributed to your code execution, that is, your personal and professional growth?
- **Error handling:** Can you identify any unhandled exceptions in your support network, that is, gaps where you need additional support or resources to accomplish your goals?
- **Function calls:** Reflect on the instances where you have called on others for support. How have these function calls enhanced your code's performance?
- **Support function:** As much as your code depends on other modules, other scripts might depend on yours. How have you served as a supporting function for others in your network? Are there more ways you can provide support?
- **Network optimization:** What are some ways to optimize your network's performance? This could be maintaining regular contact, deepening relationships, or showing appreciation to your existing connections.
- **Extending support:** In open source programming, developers freely share their code to contribute to the wider community. How can you extend your support to others in your network and broader community?
- **Transparency:** Much like an open source community, being transparent about the help you receive can empower and inspire others. How can you encourage this kind of sharing in your own network?

- **Network benefits:** Reflect on the returns your network has provided. In what ways has building a strong network influenced your personal and professional development?
- **Error logs:** Have you encountered any errors or obstacles while building your network? What strategies can you implement to overcome these bugs?
- **Updates and patches:** Based on your reflections, what specific updates can you implement to optimize your support network? Set actionable goals to expand and strengthen your network.

This code review should not only help you identify gaps in your network but also highlight its strengths. Use these reflections as a springboard to update your support code, ensuring it functions optimally for your current and future needs. Keep in mind that building a robust network, much like writing a sophisticated piece of code, is an iterative process. Happy coding!

PART

II

How to Build the Future

7

The Entrepreneurial Equation

The best way to predict the future is to create it.

—Peter Drucker

Your work is going to fill a large part of your life, and the only way to be truly satisfied is to do what you believe is great work. And the only way to do great work is to love what you do.

—Steve Jobs

EQUATIONS ARE A key component in the world of algorithms and computer science. In this chapter, we will dive into an equation that many of you might have or will embark on—the entrepreneurial equation. Before we begin this chapter, I want to provide context to the term *passion* and explain why I've chosen it as a central theme. According to the *Merriam-Webster Dictionary*, *passion* means "intense emotion compelling action," and it applies to emotions that are deeply stirring and ungovernable. When embarking on entrepreneurial endeavors, maintaining passion is vital. It's this passion that drives us to take action daily, especially when faced with challenges. It's the force that stirs our souls and pushes us beyond our limits. Passion is the key to our success; it propels us forward. Our passions typically emerge from desires to improve our lives or communities or address issues within them.

For example, I yearned for greater flexibility and more time with my family, which led me to explore freelancing. Subsequently, I discovered a passion for helping other mothers achieve the same work-life balance, inspiring me to build Allobee. However, having passion alone wasn't sufficient to reach the finish line. I needed another crucial element: technology. Acquiring knowledge and skills in tech was essential to transform my passion into a tangible product. To build the future, we must learn how to elevate our passions.

I firmly believe that the entrepreneurial equation of tech + passion applies not only to scalable start-up founders but to all businesses. Anyone who initiated a business, invested their sweat and tears in its early days, and conceived the company's idea is a founder. Regardless of the business's size, market reach, or your personal goals, the methods discussed in this book can be applied. Building isn't confined to a business's inception; it's an ongoing process. Storms may arise, damaging your business structure, requiring repair. Economic downturns or the need to pivot might occur. Building continues through every phase of a business.

Let's delve further into this entrepreneurial equation, where technology and passion converge. These two powerful forces, when combined, can ignite a revolution. They form an equation that harmonizes the logic of the digital world with the fervor of human aspirations. This chapter will explore these components and unveil their potential.

I shared previously my transformative moment when I watched a Microsoft video about setting up technology centers in developing countries. This revelation flipped a switch in my mind, demonstrating that technology could be harnessed for good. I've spent years discovering individuals and companies that merge technology and their passion to create positive change. Using technology doesn't necessarily mean becoming a coder overnight. It could involve leveraging automation tools to expedite business processes and reduce costs. Alternatively, it might mean collaborating with developers to bring your product to life or tapping into existing technology to support benevolent causes. Technology can be a powerful force for good when applied correctly.

Discovering your passion to complement technology often arises from personal experiences. For me, it stemmed from the need for flexible work as a new mom, and my realization that many others shared this need. This ignited my passion to assist mothers in accessing flexible work arrangements, eventually leading me to launch a tech start-up that combined my tech knowledge with my newfound passion. In Chapter 8, we'll explore idea generation in depth for those uncertain about their passions.

Tech and Passion, and How They Interact

Now, let's dissect this equation. Technology, at its core, is a toolbox filled with endless possibilities. It's the coding language that translates human commands into digital actions, the device that shrinks vast distances through the click of a button, or the software that transforms raw data into meaningful patterns.

Passion, however, serves as the catalyst that ignites our spirits, the unwavering force propelling us beyond the ordinary. It's the driving energy that compels us to innovate, create, and slowly change the world.

When these two powerful forces—tech and passion—intersect, the result is nothing short of exponential. Technology equips our passions with tools to turn dreams into tangible realities. In return, our passions provide purpose to technology, molding it into solutions that truly matter. When this equation finds balance, the world reaps the benefits. It's this equation that empowers us to shape the future according to our desires.

Technology and Passion Drive Innovation and Foster Positive Societal Impact

Consider any field that sparks your passion—whether it's health care, education, art, or the environment. Today, technology's reach extends to nearly every sector. Wearable devices monitor health vitals, online platforms democratize education, digital tools craft artistic masterpieces, and AI models predict climate patterns. Technology seamlessly integrates into these domains and many more. Personally, I transitioned into tech after a career in the non-profit sector because I saw the immense potential technology held for helping people and creating a better world. Regardless of where your passion lies, technology can likely become your ally, bolstering your endeavors and amplifying your impact.

Passion fuels persistence. It's the driving force behind our continuous exploration, experimentation, resilience in the face of failure, and our determination to try again. It propels us to question the status quo and venture into uncharted territories, thereby paving the way for innovation.

When passion aligns with technology, it catalyzes the creation of solutions that not only showcase innovation but also deliver tangible impact. This passionate drive has led to ground-breaking technological advancements that have transformed societies. From collaborative platforms that have revolutionized work dynamics to medical breakthroughs that have extended human longevity and improved our quality of life, technology harnessed through passion has created significant positive change.

The Synergy of Tech and Passion: My Entrepreneurial Equation

At a pivotal moment in my life, craving more than the confines of a 9-to-5, I turned to freelancing as a gateway to balance. It was here that my passion found its partner in technology—I was not an expert at programming but I was "just dangerous enough" with it to forge a new path. This synergy led to the creation of Allobee, a platform aimed at empowering mothers like me, seeking professional flexibility. Although my expertise was not in tech, my rudimentary skills were the catalyst for transformation.

I coded our initial minimal viable product, but as Allobee grew, I brought in engineers and interns to handle the technical aspects. However, my tech knowledge enabled me to communicate effectively with them. I knew how to structure our product, write technical requirements, and knew how the complexity should unfold. This knowledge saved us hours of development time and resources.

Being "dangerous enough" in coding, as I like to say, isn't about becoming a coding wizard. It's about having a functional understanding of tech, enough to appreciate its power and potential. It's about being able to collaborate with developers, ask the right questions, and make informed decisions.

In Chapters 8 and 9, I'll delve deeper into this concept and provide insights into how you can acquire the tech knowledge you need, even if you're not a technical expert. Remember, this knowledge isn't just vital at the start; it isn't just an equation. It's a compass guiding you throughout your entrepreneurial journey, using digital advancements to amplify your passion-fueled endeavors and drive societal transformation.

In the course of writing this book and engaging in numerous conversations, I've come to a powerful realization: Women have been building the future for centuries. They build for their communities and for humanity, often behind the scenes, driven not by fame but by a desire for a better future for their families and society at large.

With the advent of the internet and computers, women have added a new dimension to the way the future is being constructed. Although men have dominated this space historically, there are remarkable women who have made significant contributions, often without receiving the recognition they deserve. I've already introduced the fabulous five, who significantly shaped the advent of technology. Their contributions were instrumental to the tech field, yet their achievements were overshadowed by their male counterparts.

In the next section I will share the interview with two modern technical women who joined forces to build together: Sara Mauskopf and Anne Halsall, the founders of Winnie, a marketplace for childcare built on powerful data systems and backed by a trusted community of parents and providers. This interview was so insightful that I couldn't select just a few quotes; instead, I present it in its entirety.

Building Together: The Inspiring Partnership of Sara Mauskopf and Anne Halsall

In the following interview with Sara Mauskopf and Anne Halsall, the founders of Winnie, we delve into their extraordinary journey and how their partnership has shaped their lives and the childcare industry.

Brooke: I'm fascinated by how both of you, despite your unique backgrounds, found common ground. I'm eager to understand how your partnership evolved over the nearly eight years you've been together. How has working side-by-side shaped both of you?

Sara: When I decided to start Winnie, Anne was at the forefront of my mind. I saw her as someone exceptionally gifted and possessing raw talent that I wanted to harness. Every idea she shared was innovative, and she had an uncanny ability to execute them effortlessly. But beyond our skills and talents, what made our partnership last was our complementary nature. While Anne thrives on vision and curiosity, I'm driven by goals and achievements. The amalgamation of our distinctive traits has given us a unique dynamic, helping us continuously move toward our primary objective: aiding families in finding childcare and supporting childcare providers.

Anne: Reflecting on our journey makes me emotional. It's not just about the business; it's about the bond we've formed. Before Sara, I had never shared such an impactful working relationship with another woman. Although I had the skills and had worked with some of the best in the tech industry, it was with Sara that I found purpose and direction. Our dynamic is genuine. We don't shy away from disagreements; instead, we use them to fine-tune our ideas. There's no room for ego in our discussions, and it's this foundation of trust and respect that's made us effective leaders for our company.

Sara: To add to that, having someone as intellectually stimulating as Anne by my side has been a blessing. There's a difference between appearing intelligent and genuinely being insightful. With Anne, I found a partner who truly challenges and complements my thought process.

Anne: The feeling is mutual, Sara. Over the years, I've switched interests, but the thrill of brainstorming with Sara, tackling varied challenges, and navigating through the different phases of our business has kept me engaged.

Sara: Precisely, Anne. The challenges and products we dealt with seven years ago are vastly different from today, and that's what keeps our journey ever-evolving and exciting.

Brooke: Navigating challenges together fosters growth. As a technical founder myself, I find it difficult to connect with others who understand the nuances of being a woman, a mother, and a tech leader. Have you encountered this issue? And can you share a significant lesson you've learned as women and mothers building a tech company?

Anne: Absolutely. The cofounder relationship should be treated like a marriage. It's paramount to have unwavering trust and to always support each other. We've seen cofounder pairs dissolve, which often spells the end for start-ups. Our shared experience as women, mothers, and minorities in tech, in many ways, brought us closer. We've had disagreements, but we've always prioritized our unity, and that's been fundamental to our business.

Sara: Adding to that, we intentionally built our company to align with our lives, rather than the stereotypical start-up grind. We've been working at this for seven and a half years, and now we are finally seeing substantial revenue and profit. We've created a sustainable work-life balance, not only for ourselves but for our employees as well. For instance, our VP of engineering, who is a woman, has been with us since the beginning.

Brooke: That's impressive and commendable. You've built a company on your terms and found success, which is truly inspiring. How do you envision the future of childcare and the role that technology can play in this sector, given your position as pioneers?

Sara: This is massive. Childcare is essential for a functioning economy and for enabling women to stay in the workforce. We aim to make childcare and early education significantly more accessible and affordable. We spend considerable effort at Winnie to uplift childcare providers and educators, who are essential but underpaid.

Anne: It's a profound problem. I'm frustrated when people label this a "niche" issue. We are talking about the future of humanity, and this issue has immense social and economic implications. Unlike many in tech, who focus heavily on the technological future, we are committed to improving the social future. Early educators are shaping the lives of future generations. I want the tech industry to recognize this as a significant issue and allocate resources accordingly.

Finishing this interview, I couldn't help but think about how rare and special Sara and Anne's partnership is. Finding a technical woman to build with is akin to finding a unicorn. What these two extraordinary women have achieved together is a testament to the power of setting aside ego and combining your passion with technical knowledge to create something extraordinary.

Investors told them that they had no competitors and that they would not succeed. Eight years later, they are still here, building an amazing and needed product that is profitable. Women build for the future and humanity, and it seems to be working. Maybe not at the breakneck pace at all costs, but it works. Sara and Anne's story does not have to be unique. Women can build together, gain technical knowledge and skills, and create companies that live out their values and last for the long term.

I believe when we combine knowledge with passion, we can be successful in building the future. When we add in technical knowledge, it gives us an edge to carry us even further. Many companies are built to solve a problem, but that problem could be to get your burrito faster, not necessarily to help humanity. From working and speaking with many women building the future over the years, I have found that these women are building products and companies that they believe deeply in because they know it will truly help people. They know they are building a better future.

Embracing Values: The Final Piece of the Entrepreneurial Equation

In the journey of building the future through the entrepreneurial equation of tech and passion, there's a secret sauce that can elevate your endeavors to a whole new level: values and empathy. Women lead differently from men, and it's time to embrace this as our superpower.

Reflecting on my own entrepreneurial journey, one thing that stood out was how the years from 2019 to 2021 were the times when I was completely immersed in my passion. My values were closely aligned with what I was building, and this soulful alignment resonated with our clients, freelancers, and my team. They could feel the authenticity of our mission. We even codified our values into what we called our BeeAttitudes, fostering a sense of unity and purpose within our company:

BEE Kind

BEE Helpful

BEE Happy

BEE Mindful

BEE Curious

BEE Inclusive

BEE Bold

BEE Humble

BEE Honest

BEE Proactive

BEE Always learning

BEE Accountable

We held monthly meetings when we shared our vision, not just with our team but with our freelancers, forging a sense of community. During this time, we soared. We launched Allobee out of beta during the early months of the COVID-19 pandemic. We hosted a summit that brought together more than 600 moms from around the world and featured more than 20 incredible mom leaders in business. This momentum enabled us to raise our initial round of funding, securing $500K in just a few months at the end of 2020.

But as 2021 ended and we prepared to kick off fundraising in 2022, a shift occurred. Our focus shifted to metrics and numbers for fundraising, and internal team issues started to surface. The hardest part about being a founder and CEO is that you have to appear like everything is great to the outside world, even if the internal is crumbling. There is no way around it because when you are fundraising you cannot appear to be weak. Some of the internal issues were that one of our team members was ready to make more money and we had not raised enough yet. Because we were unable to provide that for her, I knew she might leave. Another team member decided to pull back to part time and that left more for me to take over. A few team members were just not getting along well and I should have stepped in sooner. I was so preoccupied with the raise and product development that I didn't manage these issues as effectively as I should have. I believe in extreme ownership as a leader, and I take responsibility for how the rest of 2022 unfolded. This affected our ability to raise funds, along with the economic environment and the challenges female founders face in securing funding. I share this because I believe founders need to know that everything is not great during building a start-up; we make a lot of mistakes along the way.

Somewhere along the way, I lost my deep connection with the company's values and mission. External input began to contradict my intuition, which is something they don't teach in business school but is a potent tool. My intuition was telling me to start fundraising in 2021, to maintain our focus on moms, and more. I ignored it, and that had consequences. I obviously could not predict the economic future and what the markets would do in 2022 and the slow down and shift of investor funding, but we were trying to raise in the midst of that, and if I had listened to my intuition to start sooner maybe we would have raised the round.

I also should have gone at fundraising alone on the second round and not have involved other members of my team. I did not realize how much of an impact that would have on investors and I got feedback that they only wanted to hear from the founder. One area that I pushed away from focusing on even though my gut told me to was on our community and freelancers. I pushed too hard on getting new clients for jobs that I lost a lot of the connection with our freelancers and that hurt us in the end. The issue was the community. Although membership numbers were rising it was not where we were going to make the big jumps in revenue, and I felt I needed to show investors the big jumps. I learned so much from my time building Allobee, and I really have no regrets, just knowledge to help me when I build again.

Throughout 2022, I think not only had I lost my soul connection with the company, but our freelancers and clients could feel it, too. This is something rarely discussed by founders, especially women. We often hesitate to show vulnerability in business, fearing it might put us at a disadvantage compared to our male counterparts. However, it might be what sets us apart as empathetic, intuitive leaders. It's time we embrace these strengths rather than shying away from them.

As you embark on your journey of passion and building, I encourage you to define your values and share them with your team and customers. People want to align themselves with companies whose values resonate with their own. It not only helps you lead and stay true to your values but also fosters a company with loyal and like-minded customers. In the end, this combination of values, passion, and technology forms the true equation to build a better future, one that aligns with your vision and values.

Code Review: Enhancing Your Entrepreneurial Equation

In this chapter, we explored the essence of the entrepreneurial equation, emphasizing the fusion of tech and passion to fuel innovation and drive positive societal impact. Just as in software development, where code needs regular scrutiny and debugging, our entrepreneurial equation also requires periodic review, refinement, and optimization to ensure it remains robust and effective.

Code Review Checklist

- **Tech and passion synergy:** Reflect on your understanding of the entrepreneurial equation—the confluence of technology and passion. How have you harnessed these forces in your journey so far? Are there areas where you can strengthen this synergy?
- **Passion-compelled action:** Consider your level of passion in your entrepreneurial endeavors. Is it genuinely stirring and compelling action, or has it waned over time? Reflect on strategies to reignite and maintain this vital force within you.
- **Scalable versus non-scalable:** Ponder the applicability of the entrepreneurial equation beyond scalable start-ups. Are you recognizing the potential in your own ventures, regardless of their scale? How might you incorporate the equation into your current business, no matter the size or industry?
- **Technology as a catalyst:** Revisit your relationship with technology. Are you using its power to support your entrepreneurial goals? Reflect on whether you've embraced automation, coding skills, or existing technologies effectively to accelerate your progress.
- **Passion source:** Investigate the origin of your passion. Has it evolved from personal needs or problems you've encountered? Assess whether your passion remains aligned with your initial vision and consider how this alignment can be maintained.
- **Technical knowledge as a tool:** Reflect on your technical knowledge and its role in your entrepreneurial journey.

Have you been "dangerous enough" with technology to drive your projects effectively? Think about how this knowledge can be leveraged further.

- **Tech and passion-driven innovation:** Consider the areas of passion that spark your interest, such as health care, education, or the environment. How have you explored technology's role in these fields? Reflect on examples where technology has seamlessly integrated with these passions to drive innovation.

- **Persistence and innovation:** Reflect on your entrepreneurial persistence. How has your passion-driven approach facilitated your ability to innovate, even in the face of challenges? Think about times when your tenacity led to breakthroughs.

- **Building together:** Delve into the concept of co-building with like-minded individuals. Have you considered partnerships with fellow female entrepreneurs to strengthen your ventures? Reflect on the benefits and potential challenges of such partnerships.

Code Review Outcomes

Just as we debug code to optimize its performance, this review process is designed to optimize your approach to entrepreneurship. The insights you gain will empower you to navigate your entrepreneurial equation more effectively, driving greater innovation and societal impact.

Remember that the true value of this review lies in its actionable insights. Commit to applying these insights to your entrepreneurial journey, reinforcing your passion, technical knowledge, and commitment to building a brighter future. This iterative approach to entrepreneurship ensures that your equation remains dynamic, effective, and attuned to the ever-changing landscape of innovation and technology.

8

She Innovates

Building from Idea to MVP

Boys are taught to be brave, while girls are taught to be perfect.
—Reshma Saujani

I VIVIDLY RECALL THE day when I found myself engrossed in the paperwork for my first patent. I was collaborating closely with our chief scientist, Niki Gitinabard, blending my innovative idea with her expertise in machine learning. It was an exhilarating journey, but it also highlighted an unfortunate reality—the rarity of two women coming together to build and innovate on the technical front. I couldn't help but reflect on the trailblazing women like Marie Curie and Grace Hopper, who made remarkable strides in innovation; yet, their accomplishments were exceptions in a landscape still heavily dominated by men.

Research reveals that the gender gap and discrimination are major roadblocks to women's participation in innovation. Even Marie Curie faced discrimination and was denied entrance to the French Academy of Sciences purely because she was a woman. I can't help but wonder how many women with ingenious ideas embarked on the path of innovation but were thwarted by societal expectations that pigeonholed them into predefined roles, particularly as caregivers. The lack of accessible childcare remains a significant hurdle for women today, affecting their ability to pursue innovative endeavors. As I completed that patent application, I couldn't ignore the privilege it represented, and the responsibility it carried. I fervently hope that one day my daughter and others like her will feel empowered to innovate freely. This experience prompted me to reflect on how we can genuinely create an environment that not only encourages women to innovate but also actively supports them in their journey.

The annals of history are replete with stories of women who made groundbreaking innovations, only for their contributions to be overshadowed by societal expectations and a persistent data gap. Recently, I stumbled on a remarkable story that left an indelible mark on my mind. It shed light on a lesser-known aspect of history: women at the forefront of coding. These women played pivotal roles in programming some of the earliest computers during WWII as part of the ENIAC project. They ingeniously learned to emulate the functions of a computer to subsequently program it. Interestingly, many of them were former secretaries, well-versed in processes, procedures, and meticulous attention to detail, which proved to be invaluable skills in their new roles. Tragically, their contributions have been unjustly omitted from the annals of computer science history. Fortunately, Kathy Kleiman's book, *Proving Ground: The Untold Story of the Six Women Who Programmed the World's First Modern Computer*, and the documentary she coproduced, have resurrected their stories. These women, alongside their male counterparts, were at the forefront of innovation, quite literally writing the code for the future. Their tale serves as a powerful reminder that women have always played a significant role in pushing the boundaries of innovation. It fuels my passion to continually refine my programming skills and share this knowledge with others because, as history demonstrates, women who code can indeed redefine the limits of innovation.

As a mother of two young children, I can attest that finding time for innovation amid the responsibilities of motherhood is a formidable challenge. Many have asked me how I managed to navigate this terrain, and although there's no one-size-fits-all answer, I do have insights that have proven effective for me and many others. The stories of these forgotten women innovators and my own experiences underscore the urgency of addressing the gender gap in innovation. In this chapter, we will delve into what it takes to be an innovator, especially from a woman's perspective, and explore the essential steps to transition from a novel idea to a minimum viable product (MVP). As you embark on this journey, remember that although ideas are the seeds of innovation, it's your passion, dedication, and relentless pursuit of perfection that will nurture them to fruition. Together, let's navigate this path, uncovering the secrets of innovation and mastering the art of translating ideas into impactful MVPs.

I believe that one of the key factors enabling my entrepreneurial journey was having a supportive spouse and embracing the concept of fair play, as described in the book *Fair Play* by Eve Rodsky. This approach helped us distribute the responsibilities and unseen labor of motherhood more equitably, freeing me to pursue my entrepreneurial dreams. However, it wasn't solely about a balanced division of tasks; it was also about having a partner who doubled as my most enthusiastic cheerleader and advisor.

Another area that I strongly believe could empower women is for society to fully embrace nonlinear career paths, including breaks and transitions. The journey to building might look different for women than men, often influenced by factors such as parenthood or the extended time it takes to progress in careers. In my case, the building phase coincided with the chaotic early days of mothering two young children. However, this timing eventually turned out to be an advantage. When my company began to gain momentum, my children had started school, offering me the flexibility that a traditional job couldn't provide. I've met many mothers who embarked on their building journeys while their children were young, and I think this trend emerges from the fact that the traditional workforce isn't designed to accommodate mothers effectively.

One individual who eloquently discusses this and shares valuable resources is Neha Ruch, from Mother Untitled, the place for *ambitious women* leaning into *family life*. She recently shared a profound quote on redefining ambition:

> I made a six-figure salary by 24, went to the best business school in the world at 27, and got my "dream title" at 29. I never felt more ambition than the day I chose to pause my career for family life. And again, a year later, when I started a "passion project." And again, when I paused to grow as a mother to two. And again, when I asked for help so I could grow this business at 37. Ambition isn't your schooling, your title, or your salary. It's the constant and deliberate aligning of your actions with the life you want to live. It's redefining your work of meaning to you. And above all, it's trusting yourself.

Trusting oneself is perhaps the most powerful thing a woman can do. As I've internalized this lesson, I've felt an increasing sense of empowerment. To truly support women in innovation and building, universal childcare is essential. I recognize that not every woman wants to have children, so the need runs deeper than that. It's about acknowledging that care, in all its forms, is fundamental to shaping a better future for humanity. My friend, Blessing Adesiyan, is a work care evangelist who has dedicated herself to this cause after leaving her own corporate career. Her work focuses on helping companies prioritize care, which is essential because we must revolutionize how we treat our employees; otherwise, the mental health crisis and burnout will persist and worsen. Caring for one another enables all of us to thrive. Moreover, as the baby boomer generation ages, many of their adult children will soon face the dual responsibilities of caring for both children and aging parents. The care crisis will only escalate unless we take concrete steps to address it.

Over the years, many people have asked me how I managed to focus and stay present while building my company, given the daily distractions of motherhood. There's a prevailing perception that innovators must possess an almost maniacal level of focus, which many believe mothers can't attain. Personally, I view motherhood as my superpower, the catalyst that ignited my innovative spirit. Bringing a child into this world has a unique way of inspiring one to make it better. I'd do anything for my children, and that includes being intensely committed to creating a brighter future for them.

Certainly, time management is crucial, but as a mother, I learned to master the art of time blocking and effective time management out of sheer necessity. If I was going to be a mother and a professional, I had no other choice. I've come to realize that when you combine audacious dreams and a clear mission with unwavering determination, you can achieve the seemingly impossible. For instance, as I've mentioned, I ended up waking up at 4:30 every weekday morning the summer I wrote this book, a far-from-ideal routine that required significant physical and mental adjustment. However, my aspiration to write this book was so compelling that it pushed me to show up and make it happen. I knew that securing the book contract in April meant I was in for an intense journey to complete the manuscript by September. Yet, I was confident that with a well-structured plan and my existing skill set, I could achieve it. When we deeply desire something and are driven by the entrepreneurial equation, we can surmount seemingly insurmountable obstacles.

My children have been profound teachers in my life, constantly challenging me to become a better version of myself. Recently, my daughter expressed anxiety about the start of PE at school, a situation that transported me back to my own childhood, when I would feign illness to avoid physical education. I resolved never to let my daughter inherit such self-limiting belief as I once had, so I sat her down, and we discussed the positive aspects of PE, emphasizing how fortunate we are to be able to move our bodies. We celebrated the power of her body, her dedication at soccer practice, and her upcoming 5K run with me. We also discussed the practical tools she could use if anxiety struck, like having two water bottles at the ready and employing deep breathing techniques. Her anxiety lifted, and she left for school eagerly anticipating PE, returning later that day to declare it her new favorite subject. This experience reinforced the immense power of mindset and the words we tell ourselves.

For years, I had convinced myself that I was bad at math, echoing the beliefs I'd inherited from my parents. They too considered themselves inept at math, so I assumed it was an inherent family trait. Consequently, I approached math classes with a sense of inevitability: I could never get it right. I associated math with computer science and programming, until my husband showed me that it was much more than that, and it wasn't as daunting as I had believed. I pursued and obtained a master's degree and ventured into product development, recognizing that my analytical mind, propensity for cause-and-effect thinking, strong process orientation, and innate curiosity were valuable assets in learning how to code.

I believe that women operate in cyclical patterns, largely influenced by our unique body cycles. This topic is something I want to delve into more toward the end of this book because it's a crucial hack that has enabled me to continue building as both a woman and a mother. For now, I want to emphasize that we aren't designed to build 24/7, year after year. If we attempt to do so, we risk burnout, and even the most brilliant ideas will wither away. To enable women to truly shape the future, we must embrace our distinctive operational rhythms, understanding that this uniqueness is a superpower. However, it may not always align with the traditional model of innovation. This is precisely why I wrote this book: to share with fellow women that it's not only possible to build a brighter future but also that we can achieve it by approaching it with a slight twist and by working together. So, let's now dive into how you can discover the idea that will be your contribution to building a better future.

I've guided you through my GEMS framework, shared how I ventured into the tech field, and began my journey of building. However, one aspect I haven't touched on yet is how to actually build. Many of you reading this might already be involved in some form of building, whether it's side projects, side hustles, or taking on extra initiatives, often regardless of whether you consider yourself an entrepreneur. I've found that this inclination stems from a mix of societal influences and the fact that women are, at heart, innovators. According to research from *Harvard Business Review*, there are five defining characteristics that set innovators apart (https://hbr.org/2013/10/the-five-character istics-of-successful-innovators). However, the most defining factor that distinguishes a creative individual from an innovator is execution. Here are these five characteristics, and I encourage you to reflect on whether you see yourself in any of them:

- **Opportunistic mindset:** Innovators are skilled at spotting gaps in the market and addressing user pain points. Many opportunists thrive on new and complex experiences, and interestingly, several have been found to exhibit traits associated with ADHD. ADHD can come with some negative traits such as being easily distracted, having a hard time focusing, and more, but it also can come with some super-powers that include hyper-focus moments, risk-taking, multi-passionate, high energy, and creative mindset. Although I haven't been formally diagnosed, I've recognized similar traits in myself and have employed various strategies associated with ADHD to support my building.

- **Formal education or training:** Contrary to the image of drop-out geniuses, most innovators have deep educational backgrounds or extensive training. This deep knowledge is essential in distinguishing between relevant and irrelevant information.

- **Proactivity and persistence:** Persistence drives innovators to capitalize on opportunities they identify. Effective innovators are often highly motivated, resilient, and energetic individuals.

- **More cautious than most:** Contrary to the stereotype of risk-taking entrepreneurs, successful innovators tend to be more organized, cautious, and risk averse. This perspective might diverge from the traditional start-up ethos, which often prioritizes scaling at all costs and embracing risk. It raises an intriguing question about whether genuine innovation can flourish within the traditional start-up venture model.

- **Social capital:** Innovators harness their connections and networks to acquire resources and build strong alliances. Remember the importance of support from Chapter 6? Networking and building a robust support system are invaluable for innovators. Having social capital to draw on is an immense asset.

Now, you might be thinking, "I possess most of these characteristics or know people who do, but they're not innovators." First, it's possible that execution is lacking. But the real secret sauce lies in the entrepreneurial equation, combined with a meaningful mission and a clear vision. The desire to innovate or build something meaningful is another critical component, and it's not a universal drive.

I've always been an idea person. I can generate ideas endlessly when I'm in the zone. I've amassed a notebook filled with concepts I may revisit someday because I can't execute all the ideas I generate. This creative wellspring has been pivotal in my ability to innovate and iterate rapidly. My husband often teases me about my constant flow of ideas, but I concur with him. Allobee was the idea that stuck, not just because it was an idea but because it was coupled with a mission to help women receive fair compensation for flexible work. That mission fueled my determination to build.

If you don't currently see yourself as an innovator or consider yourself an idea person, don't be discouraged. A decade ago, if you'd asked me whether I'd consider myself an innovator, leading a company that would eventually be acquired, I'd have dismissed the idea as absurd. I believe that a significant hurdle for women in building and innovating is overcoming our self-doubt and limited self-belief. Self-belief and trust are where the power and grit emerge, propelling us forward on the path to success. It took a significant amount of self-work and a superb support system for me to reach where I am today. I'm convinced that I always possessed this tenacity, curiosity, confidence, persistence, and determination as a child, but somewhere along the way, societal norms for women chipped away at these qualities.

You might not perceive yourself as an innovator today, but I'd like to challenge you to finish this book. Take the knowledge you gain, engage in the activities it contains, and see if it ignites some ideas and momentum. If you're reading this book, you likely possess a spark within you that beckoned you here. If you're already building and some sections of this chapter seem irrelevant for now, feel free to skip ahead. However, I believe you'll find value in these words. So, let's dive in, and I'll guide you through what I've learned about the art of building and innovating.

Where It Starts: The Idea

Writing a guide that's very industry-specific would be impossible, but I've discovered core principles that work across all industries during my journey of building and growing Allobee. Our product had an industry-agnostic client base, and our freelancers came from diverse backgrounds. However, they all shared similar pain points and needs. Thus, this guide can be applied to kickstart any idea, and that's where we'll begin. It's worth noting that ideas aren't just essential at the outset of building a product; they remain vital long term because you might need to pivot or make significant shifts in your business.

My ideas journal is my go-to resource when I'm not feeling particularly creative or inspired. It's a place where I revisit ideas I've had over the years, assessing if there's something I want to tackle. Sometimes these ideas are simple and unrelated to my current primary project, but they might become a side project or a venture I decide to explore. Often, our best ideas strike us at rather inconvenient times, like in the middle of a product sprint or during a vacation. These aren't the moments to dive headfirst into building and testing. However, it's crucial to capture those ideas, and I suggest you get a notebook or find a digital way that works for you to capture these. I use the Notes app on my iPhone to jot down ideas on the go, and my husband does the same. We often generate ideas during long car rides when we're engaged in deep conversations with fewer distractions, and we make sure to record them for later. Even before you begin building, things can go awry. I've collaborated with numerous founders, and I've identified four major mistakes people make during the idea phase:

- **The guise of awesome:** Founders sometimes believe they must have an incredible, "wow factor" idea to get started. Interestingly, many of the most profitable start-ups began with seemingly mundane concepts. Even groundbreaking innovations of our time often appeared unremarkable at their inception. For instance, Google was the 20th search engine, and Facebook was far from the first social network. The key is starting with a good enough idea and then focusing on execution, which is the crux of innovation and what distinguishes the greats.

- **Head first on the first idea:** Rushing into the first idea that pops into your mind is often the wrong approach. Although you might revisit this idea and develop it further after exploring other options, it's crucial not to jump in blindly. In my experience, Allobee, in the form it would eventually become, was not my initial idea. I had initially contemplated building a company similar to Postmates but for local organic food, which I named Queen City Roots. This idea did not pan out and eventually I let it go. When testing an idea, I like to spend some time with it, asking myself if I'm still interested after a week or two. Remember, bringing an idea to life is a lengthy process, so you'd better enjoy it. Also, keep in mind that the idea is just a starting point; ideas can evolve and change over time.

- **Problems are the key:** Starting with a solution is a common mistake. It often means you're not addressing real user pain points. An idea should stem from a problem, and you should build the solution after gaining a deep understanding of the problem's complexity.

- **Ideas are hard to find:** They're not! You just need to start paying attention to people's problems and pain points. Look in Reddit channels, Facebook groups, on social media, and spend time with people, listening. Once you find one problem, you'll start noticing them all around you, and you'll begin to maintain an ideas journal.

Let's Find an Idea

Now that you know what to avoid during the ideas phase, let's embark on the exciting journey of finding that idea that could potentially set the course for your start-up's success. Just as in programming, where the initial logic or algorithm forms the foundation on which all subsequent lines of code are written, in the world of start-ups, the idea is the genesis of everything. It's the spark that ignites the flame, determining the trajectory of an entire enterprise, along with its triumphs and trials. Next, we'll delve into seven core strategies to kindle that spark, but before we dive in I want to remind you that this process could take a few days to months, so do not rush it. Block some time on your calendar for idea generation and pick two or three of the following strategies to dive into at a sitting.

The Unfair Advantage
- Leverage what your team (or you!) excel at.
- Reflect on every company or internship you've been a part of.
- Extract unique insights, identify broken systems, or highlight in-house tools.
- *Example:* Mixpanel emerged from advanced analytics tools initially developed at Slide.

Self-Service Solutions
- Ponder solutions for personal problems.
- Contemplate daily life inefficiencies.
- *Example:* DoorDash was born out of a personal need for food delivery.

Conceptualize Ideas Rooted in Long-Term Passions
- List topics or industries you're genuinely enthusiastic about.
- Evaluate their feasibility as start-up ventures.

- *Example*: SpaceX, was founded on Elon Musk's unwavering passion for space exploration.

Riding the Wave of Change
- Recognize and capitalize on current world changes.
- Acknowledge recent technological or regulatory shifts.
- *Example*: Zoom, which capitalized on the surging demand for remote communication tools, was notably accelerated by the pandemic.

Iterating the Proven
- Seek improvements to successful business models.
- Identify and develop variants or extensions.
- *Example*: Uber revolutionized the taxi industry with its app-based ride-hailing service.

The Crowdsourced Approach
- Generate ideas through collective wisdom.
- Engage with peers and fellow start-up founders for valuable feedback.
- Identify recurring patterns or issues that require solutions.
- *Example*: Reddit is a platform built on the collective wisdom of internet users where content is created and curated by the community.

The Broken Industry Paradigm
- Target industries yearning for disruption.
- Identify sectors perceived as outdated or inefficient.
- *Example*: Airbnb set its sights on the hospitality industry, providing a fresh alternative to traditional hotels and accommodations.

In the coding world, the foundational algorithm is crucial. Similarly, in the start-up realm, the initial idea holds paramount importance. As you embark on your start-up journey, remember that although ideas serve as the seedlings, it's your passion, dedication, and continuous refinement that nurture them to fruition. So, as you contemplate these strategies, let your idea take center stage, and allow the magic to unfold from there.

What Is Your Unique Solution to This Idea?

You might already have an idea brewing in your mind, or perhaps one has started to take shape. Now, the crucial step is ensuring that the problem you're aiming to solve has a distinctive and viable solution. My journey with Allobee didn't begin as a curated freelance marketplace for women seeking flexible work; it initially revolved around the concept of a women's economy. I wanted to empower women by facilitating connections and payments, inspired by my experience in the coworking space I helped establish. This concept evolved further as I ventured into freelancing and collaborated with solopreneurs and small business owners.

By this point, I had combined elements of the long-term passions with my freelance and coworking experiences, all while riding the wave of change. I had observed a significant number of educated women leaving the workforce, women who still desired to make an impact and earn money. Additionally, I recognized an opportunity to iterate on the proven models like UpWork, this time with a focus on women and small businesses. However, as I delved deeper into evaluating my idea, I realized that adjustments were necessary to truly meet users' needs.

Idea Evaluation

The process of idea evaluation can vary widely, ranging from a few days to several years. It's important not to compare your time line with others, as every idea and founder is unique, influenced by various factors. In the case of Allobee, it took most of the first half of 2018 to evaluate the initial concept. I proceeded to build our initial MVP during summer and early fall 2018 before launching a crowdfunding campaign later that year.

There's no single formula for evaluating an idea, and it may not entirely apply to ideas outside the traditional start-up framework. However, I believe these principles hold true across various scenarios, derived from my experiences in accelerators like OnDeck, insights from resources like Y Combinator, and interactions with numerous early-stage start-up founders. Here are some key considerations during the idea-evaluation phase:

- **How big is the idea?** Take a moment to gauge the potential size of your idea. Consider the market opportunity and total addressable market at a high level. This also prompts you to contemplate whether the idea might be too broad, possibly requiring some narrowing or niche specialization.
- **Founder and market fit?** Assess how well you fit within the context of the idea and the market. Do your experiences and connections align with this particular market? For instance, my background as a freelancer and consultant for small businesses provided a strong fit for Allobee's concept.
- **Are you sure it's a big idea?** Beyond the market size, delve into the idea's overall impact. Consider whether it's truly substantial and capable of making a significant difference. This reflection can help align your passion and motivation with the idea's potential.
- **Do you want this problem to be solved? How invested are you?** Gauge your personal investment in seeing this problem solved. Your level of commitment and passion can be a driving force as you build. For me, the need for women to be paid for flexible work was deeply personal, as I was navigating the challenges of balancing motherhood and work.

- **Are there changes in technology, the world, or new opportunities to build on?** Stay attuned to recent advancements in technology and global shifts. New tools, platforms, or cultural changes can open doors for innovation. For example, advancements in artificial intelligence and no-code solutions have created fresh opportunities in various industries.
- **Learn your filters: Rejecting or not rejecting?** Be aware of your own filters and biases when evaluating ideas. Avoid rejecting ideas simply because they seem hard, boring, or too ambitious. Sometimes, the seemingly mundane ideas can generate substantial profit and success, whereas ambitious ideas can lead to significant impact.

As you embark on the idea evaluation process, resist the temptation to jump straight into creating detailed business plans, modeling financials, or conducting exhaustive competitive analyses. These steps can come later if the idea proves viable. Instead, iterate quickly during your evaluation to see if you still resonate with the idea after considering the listed factors.

Take a Gut Check

Now that you've evaluated your idea, it's crucial to consider your vision for it. Do you aspire to disrupt industries, scale rapidly, and go big? Or do you envision building a sustainable, long-term company? Are you in this for the journey, or do you plan to sell your venture quickly? When I embarked on building Allobee, I recognized a monumental problem that required full commitment, disruption, and scaling. I made the decision to go all in, fully aware of the path ahead. However, not all ideas should follow the same trajectory. Some may not require venture funding or the traditional start-up model. This model, which often focuses on quick returns, might not always align with groundbreaking ideas aimed at shaping a better future for humanity.

The suitability of this model depends on the venture capital firm's philosophy, support, and time line expectations for returns. Although it's not always just about the money, ultimately, it does play a significant role. Therefore, the key question to ask yourself is whether this path will hinder or help your idea and the way you want to build.

I Have an Idea; Now What?

Congratulations, you've made significant progress by identifying an idea you want to pursue. Hopefully, you've spent some time reflecting on whether this idea truly resonates with you. At this stage, three common factors tend to hold many people back from moving forward: money, time, and skill set.

Frequently, founders find themselves stuck after the idea evaluation phase, especially if they lack technical skills. They worry that they must raise substantial funds to hire developers. However, this is not the time to start hiring a team. Instead, think of your idea as a fragile baby that needs nurturing and feeding to see if it starts to grow. This is where you begin building your MVP, and it doesn't necessarily require a developer or a team of developers, as many tend to believe.

Women, in particular, often reach this stage and, if they lack technical skills, may freeze or lose momentum. I've witnessed this scenario unfold far too often. In Chapter 9, I'll guide you on how to become proficient enough with coding and technology to build anything to a level where you can gain some traction. For now, all you really need is your idea and the determination to kickstart your MVP.

The MVP: The First Step in Building Your Idea

You might be wondering, what in the world is an MVP? Well, it's a product with just the basics, enough to capture the attention of early adopters and make your solution stand out. Remember, you began with a problem, and now you're providing an initial solution. Note that it doesn't have to encompass the entire solution you envision at this stage.

Why Build an MVP?

An MVP serves as a foundation that can be enhanced as you validate (or invalidate) assumptions, learn about users' needs, and develop future iterations that better serve your customers. Essentially, it's your starting point for testing whether your idea truly serves people.

I can't emphasize this enough: I've encountered countless founders who have spent a fortune building an MVP. Please, before you even think about paying someone to build anything, read this chapter and the next, and follow the steps I outline. Trust me on this. Over the years, I've helped founders save what amounts to millions of dollars because, often, nontechnical founders believe that creating an MVP or even a prototype is too daunting a task. In this book, I'm going to debunk that myth for you.

A few years ago, I conducted a workshop for students at North Carolina State University called "How to Build an MVP." I shared a comprehensive workbook with them, which you can also download from the resource guide for this book (details at the end of this book). This workbook delves into the following steps in greater detail, allowing you to thoroughly flesh out your MVP. For the purposes of this chapter, I want to emphasize the simplicity of building an MVP. Let's dive in.

Step 1: Identify and Understand Your Business and Market Needs   In this step, you want to identify your business's long-term goals. Write them down, always keeping in mind that your goals should be driven by the problem you're solving. You don't need to overcomplicate this; just ensure your goals are centered on the question of "why are we building this?"

Step 2: Map Out User Journeys Now that you have your goals, delve into the specifics of your target users. This is where you create user personas, outlining the needs, motivations, and pain points of those who will use your product. User personas are invaluable in product development and marketing. Get detailed here; strive to know everything about these users so that you truly understand their journey with your product.

After identifying the users, outline the actions they need to take within your product to achieve their goals. This exercise helps you identify opportunities and how you can add value while solving pain points. Create a list of these actions for each user.

Step 3: Create a Pain and Gain Map With user personas and actions in hand, it's time to construct a pain and gain map for each action. This map is crucial for ensuring your product effectively addresses user problems and needs. Begin by collecting data and insights from potential users, surveys, or interviews to identify their pain points, challenges, and frustrations. Categorize these issues as pain—these are the problems your MVP should aim to solve. In the gain column, list the potential benefits users expect from your product, such as increased efficiency or time savings. The pain and gain map provides a visual representation of user needs, guiding your MVP development by focusing on critical pain points and potential gains. By directly addressing these, your MVP can deliver immediate value to users and increase its chances of success. Continuously update and refine this map as you gather more user feedback and iterate on your product.

This exercise helps you pinpoint where you can most effectively resolve pain points and add gains. Concentrate on building features that address these areas for your MVP, while considering other areas for future iterations in your product road map.

Step 4: Define Success Criteria   Defining success criteria for your MVP is crucial for measuring its effectiveness. Start by setting clear, specific, and measurable goals that align with your product's purpose. These goals may include metrics such as user engagement, conversion rates, or customer satisfaction scores. Consider what success looks like in the short term—what specific outcomes indicate that your MVP is achieving its intended purpose? Additionally, think about the key performance indicators that matter most to your business. Note that success criteria can often be more than just a single metric. Collaborate with your team to define these criteria and ensure they are realistic and attainable for an MVP. Continuously monitor and analyze the data to measure your MVP's performance, and be prepared to adjust your goals and strategy based on the results to continually improve your product.

Step 5: Decide What Features to Build   Now that you have a solid foundation and a deep understanding of your business and customer needs, you're ready to identify and prioritize the features you'll build. Start by focusing on features that directly contribute to achieving your defined success metrics. Identify the core functionalities essential for addressing the pain points or needs of your target users. Lean toward simplicity; remember that the MVP is about delivering the minimum necessary to validate your idea. Collaborate closely with your development team to outline these features and ensure they align with your product's purpose. Maintain a feedback loop with your team and potential users as you build your MVP, adapting and refining your feature set as needed to increase your chances of success.

While Building the MVP: Essential Steps

During the MVP development phase, there are some essential steps you need to take to make sure you have momentum for your product once the MVP is completed. A lot of times founders forget to do these steps alongside building their initial product and that can set you up for failure if you have no one to share the product with when you are done building.

Build an Email List   Building an email list before or during your MVP development is a strategic move with significant benefits. It enables you to create a community of interested individuals who can become your earliest adopters and advocates. Through regular updates, you can keep them engaged and informed about your progress, generating excitement and anticipation for your upcoming launch. Furthermore, an email list provides a direct channel for gathering valuable feedback, conducting surveys, and refining your product based on real user insights. It's a powerful tool for building a user-centered MVP and ensuring a more successful product launch when the time comes.

Not sure where to start? Here are three simple ways to begin building your email list:

- **Create a sign-up form on your website:** Include an email sign-up form on your website's home page or landing pages. Make it prominent and easy to use, asking for minimal information such as the email address and maybe the user's first name. Explain the value of subscribing, such as receiving exclusive content, updates, or special offers.
- **Offer incentives:** Encourage people to subscribe by offering incentives, such as e-books, whitepapers, or access to webinars. Visitors are more likely to sign up when they see they'll get something valuable in return.

- **Promote on social media:** Use your social media platforms to promote your email list. Create posts and stories about the benefits of subscribing and provide a direct link to your sign-up form. Paid advertising campaigns can also help you reach a larger audience.

Remember, the key is to provide value and maintain consistency. Nurturing your subscribers by sending them relevant and engaging content over time can become a powerful tool for customer engagement and product promotion.

Build Your Brand (Personal or Company)   Starting to build your personal brand as a founder or your company's brand early on, even before your MVP launch, is a strategic move that can pay substantial dividends. It sets the stage for brand recognition and trust, which are invaluable in today's competitive landscape. Building a brand presence establishes your authority, helps you connect with your target audience, and fosters a sense of authenticity. It also makes it easier to generate interest, gain traction, and attract potential users or customers to your MVP when it's ready. Moreover, a strong brand identity can help you convey your mission, values, and the unique selling points of your product, making it more appealing and relatable to your audience. Building a brand is a long-term investment, and starting early ensures you're well positioned for success from the outset.

Here are three simple ways to get started with building your personal or company's brand before launching your MVP:

- **Content creation:** Begin creating and sharing valuable content related to your industry or niche. This could be in the form of blog posts, articles, videos, or social media posts. Share your knowledge, insights, and experiences. Consistent content creation helps position you as an authority in your field and draws an audience interested in your expertise.

- **Engage on social media:** Actively engage with your target audience on social media platforms. Participate in discussions, answer questions, and share relevant content. This not only helps you connect with potential users or customers but also showcases your commitment to your field and your willingness to engage with your audience.
- **Network and collaborate:** Attend industry events, join relevant online communities, and network with professionals in your field. Building relationships and collaborating with others in your industry can help amplify your message and reach a broader audience. It also enhances your credibility by association.

Remember that building a brand is an ongoing process, and consistency is key. Over time, these efforts will contribute to a strong and recognizable personal or company brand when you're ready to launch your MVP.

Network   Networking while developing your MVP is crucial for several reasons. First, it connects you with potential mentors, advisors, or collaborators who can provide valuable insights and guidance as you navigate the MVP development process. Second, it helps you establish connections within your industry or niche, opening doors to partnerships or early adopters for your product. Last, networking creates a support system of like-minded individuals who understand the challenges of entrepreneurship, offering encouragement and solutions when hurdles arise. Ultimately, a strong network can accelerate your MVP's success by providing resources, knowledge, and a community that shares your entrepreneurial vision.

Networking can feel daunting, especially if you are more introverted or have limited time as a founder. You can refer back to Chapter 6 for more in-depth strategies on building your network. Here are three simple ways you can begin building your network:

- **Attend industry events:** Conferences, seminars, webinars, and workshops relevant to your industry or niche are excellent opportunities to meet and connect with like-minded professionals. Actively participate, ask questions, and engage in discussions to leave a memorable impression.
- **Use social media:** Platforms like LinkedIn, Facebook, Instagram, and niche-specific forums or groups can be goldmines for networking. Share your insights, participate in conversations, and reach out to individuals who inspire you or share common interests. Personalize your messages when connecting.
- **Leverage existing contacts:** Your current contacts, whether they are friends, family, or former colleagues, can introduce you to their network. Let them know about your venture and ask for introductions to individuals who might be valuable additions to your network. Mutual connections can create instant rapport.

Consistency and a genuine interest in building relationships are key when applying these strategies to grow your network effectively. In Chapter 9, I share with you the essential tech knowledge you need to have or learn to be proficient as a builder and founder. I believe these skills can save you a lot of money, headaches, and failure while helping you become a more effective entrepreneur.

Code Review: Enhancing Your Idea Generation and MVP Development

In this chapter, our focus shifts squarely to the heart of the beginning of entrepreneurial success: idea generation and MVP development. Just as in software development, where code needs regular scrutiny and debugging, our ideas and MVPs require periodic review, refinement, and optimization to ensure they remain robust and effective. Here's a set of review questions for you to reflect on:

- **Idea generation prowess:** Reflect on your ability to generate ideas that are not just innovative but also aligned with your passion and vision. How have you honed this skill over time? Are there strategies or methods you can employ to bolster your idea generation prowess?
- **Passion-fueled ideation:** Investigate the origins of your ideas. Have they emerged from personal needs or problems you've encountered? Assess whether your ideas remain aligned with your initial passion-driven vision and explore ways to maintain this alignment.
- **MVP scalability:** Think about your current MVP or what you have planned. Have you thought through how it will scale over time? You do not need all the answers now, but it is important to see where you would need to adjust to make the changes for scale, if that is your goal.
- **Technology as an enabler:** Revisit your use of technology as a catalyst for MVP development. Are you effectively leveraging automation, coding skills, or existing technologies to accelerate your MVP project? Are you comfortable with technology, or is your discomfort holding you back? Reflect on how technology can be further integrated into your processes.
- **Complementary skills:** Analyze the synergy between your technical proficiency and the skills of your team members in MVP development. How has this collaboration shaped your MVP? Are there skills missing in your current building needs?
- **Building collaboratively:** Delve into the concept of co-building MVPs with like-minded individuals. Have you explored partnerships with fellow female entrepreneurs to strengthen your MVP? Reflect on the advantages and potential challenges of such collaborations.

As you undertake this code review focused on idea generation and MVP development, remember that the true value of this process lies in its actionable insights. These insights will empower you to navigate your entrepreneurial journey more effectively, driving greater innovation and impact through your MVP.

Just as we debug code to optimize its performance, this review process is designed to optimize your approach to idea generation and MVP development. Commit to applying these insights throughout your entrepreneurial journey, reinforcing your passion, technical knowledge, and commitment to building a brighter future. This iterative approach ensures that your ideas and MVPs remain dynamic, effective, and attuned to the ever-changing landscape of innovation and technology.

9

Just Dangerous Enough

The Power of Technical Knowledge

Everybody should learn to program a computer, because it teaches you how to think.

—Steve Jobs

Whether you want to uncover the secrets of the universe, or you just want to pursue a career in the 21st century, basic computer programming is an essential skill to learn.

—Stephen Hawking

IN THE WORLD of technology and entrepreneurship, there's an unspoken power that comes with technical knowledge. Yet, for some reason, women have often been excluded from this powerful realm. I suspect there's a reason behind this, one that stems from the realization that when women gain proficiency in coding and tech, they become forces to be reckoned with. Their empowerment and potential to change the world can be perceived as a threat by those who wish to maintain the status quo. Whether this threat is conscious or not, it exists, and it's something we must acknowledge.

Now, here's the remarkable part: many women have an innate ability to grasp coding quickly if they're introduced to it with the right mindset. Take me, for example. I've always been someone who loves processes, and my background in history ingrained in me the concept of cause and effect. When I ventured into the world of tech and decided to learn how to code, I was pleasantly surprised to find that it came more naturally to me than I had anticipated.

I have a passion for simplifying technical concepts for non-technical individuals, primarily because I was once in their shoes. Not too long ago, I was a nontechnical person, facing a steep learning curve. Back then, I often wished for someone who could break down complex tech concepts into understandable pieces. Now, I want to be that person for you. I want to share my technical knowledge in a way that's simple yet effective, demystifying the world of tech for aspiring women entrepreneurs.

When I embarked on my journey of building, I sought resources to guide me in starting a start-up. I read several books, but I couldn't help but notice that all of them were written by men. Although these books provided valuable insights, I felt that the female perspective was underrepresented. Moreover, I couldn't find a single book that laid out a clear road map for building. I had to piece together knowledge from various sources over several years to figure out what I needed to build Allobee. The technical books available were rarely authored by women, and they often lacked a start-up-focused approach.

Granted, there are aspects of building a company that differ across industries, and some processes may be more extended in certain fields. However, at the core, the principles remain the same. I want to share all the knowledge I've gained from building my first tech start-up while it's still fresh in my mind. I yearned to hear from people who were in the thick of things, not founders who had already become unicorns or those who had moved very far beyond the early days of building. The start-up journey is long, and sometimes you don't realize how early you are in the game.

Up until this point in the book, I've presented you with reasons why you should embark on this journey, shared what worked for me, guided you through idea generation, and even explained how to structure an MVP. In this chapter, we'll take the next step. It's time to begin building, and I'll provide you with the tools to do just that. I'll show you how to harness the power of coding with minimal actual coding experience. We're fortunate to live in an era when AI advancements have given us incredible tools like ChatGPT and Copilot, which can assist us in coding. You no longer need to be a coding expert or possess a computer science degree. You simply need to be "dangerous enough," meaning you have just enough technical knowledge and hacking ability that you can get your MVP out into the world yourself or with a very small team. It also transfers to supporting you throughout the whole building process not just the beginning because you will know enough to tackle technical issues that arise. In this chapter, I'll teach you how. Rest assured; I've made it straightforward. If the thought of coding makes you uneasy, I'll do my best to dispel that feeling by the end of this chapter.

Coding is a skill that has proven to be the most valuable in my career. It's not just about writing lines of code; it's about adopting a coder's thought process and problem-solving approach. The rest of this book won't turn you into a coding expert, but it will equip you with the knowledge and tools to plan and take action. If you decide to delve deeper into coding, refer to my resource guide at the end of the book, where I've compiled my top recommendations for learning how to code.

By the time you finish this chapter, my goal is for you to feel empowered to implement the knowledge and tools provided into your building journey, step-by-step. When this book concludes, you'll have all the tools (and more) to build or continue building with newfound perspectives and resources. I know I once thought coding was an insurmountable challenge, akin to facing an impenetrable math problem. But it's not, and I believe you'll discover the same.

As you dive into this chapter, remember it's perfectly okay to pause when you need to. If you're not quite ready to delve into the intricacies of building right now, feel free to skip to Chapter 10 until you are. I don't want you to get overwhelmed, but I also want you to know that technology has bestowed us with remarkable tools that can empower you to build the future. This chapter lays out these tools for you, and they'll be here whenever you're ready to explore them.

Let's Start with a Road Map

When embarking on the journey of building a product, whether you're a tech-savvy enthusiast or just beginning to delve into the world of technology, a road map or plan is your guiding star. It helps you navigate the intricate path ahead, ensuring you know where you're heading and how to get there. We've already laid the groundwork in Chapter 8, where we dived into the creative process of generating ideas and discussed the importance of an MVP (minimum viable product). Now, it's time to provide you with a comprehensive, step-by-step guide to simplify the entire process and transform your vision into reality.

Idea Validation: Bringing Your Vision to Life

The first crucial step in this journey is idea validation. It's not enough to have a brilliant concept; you need to ensure it aligns with the market and resonates with your target audience. Here's how you can validate your idea effectively:

- **Identify the problem:** Begin by gaining a crystal-clear understanding of the problem you aim to solve. This forms the bedrock of your venture.

- **Audience:** Determine the individuals or groups who face this problem and could potentially become your target users. They are the heart of your product's success.
- **Competitive analysis:** Research existing solutions in the market. How does your idea stand apart? What unique value does it bring? Understanding your competition is vital.
- **Feedback:** Don't keep your idea a secret. Share it with friends, potential customers, and mentors. Their initial feedback will provide valuable insights and help you refine your concept.

Defining Your Vision: The Blueprint for Success

Once your idea is validated and you're certain it has the potential to thrive, it's time to define your product vision. This step is all about clarity. Your vision must be articulated in such a way that it becomes your guiding light throughout the development process. I do not want you to overthink it at this point. You do not need to be using super fancy tools or making this overcomplicated. You could put everything into a Notion workspace and categorize based off the section and then link outward to other tools. I have mentioned several tools throughout that I have used and that have worked well. Most have free trials or are affordable, so do not worry about spending a lot of money on this phase. If you want to see more how I have created MVPs with various tools, please head over to the resources section at the back of the book and check out our site filled with tutorials.

Now let's dive in on how to do it:

- **High-level overview:** Start by crafting a concise and straightforward description of your product's primary goal or purpose. Think of it as the North Star that keeps you on course.
- **Scope:** Determine the must-have features, the core functionalities, and the nice-to-have ones. It's essential to prioritize your features wisely, avoiding the pitfall of feature creep by focusing on the essentials first.

Designing the User Experience: Crafting a Seamless Journey

A great idea and a clear vision are just the beginning. Your product's user experience (UX) plays a pivotal role in its success. This step is about designing how users will interact with your creation. Here's how you can craft an exceptional UX:

- **User personas:** Create detailed profiles of your ideal users. These fictional characters will guide your design and feature decisions, ensuring they cater to your audience's needs and preferences.
- **User journey mapping:** Plot out the complete journey of a user interacting with your product, from their initial contact to their final interaction. Understanding their experience is crucial for a successful design.
- **Wireframing:** You don't need to be a design expert to begin this process. Start with basic layouts of your product's interface using tools such as Balsamiq or even pen-and-paper sketches. Canva also makes wireframing easy these days, as well as their drawing tools. The goal is to visualize the structure without diving into intricate details.

Designing the User Interface: Bringing Your Vision to Life

With the user experience in place, it's time to focus on the user interface. This is where the visual appeal and functionality of your product come together. Here's how you can tackle this phase:

- **Mood boards:** Collect designs, colors, fonts, and images that resonate with your product's intended look and feel. Mood boards serve as visual inspiration. You can make these easily with Canva.
- **Prototyping:** Create interactive prototypes using tools such as Figma, Adobe XD, or InVision. Depending on the

complexity of your product you might be able to use something as simple as Squarespace or Webflow as drag-and-drop sites to help bring your vision to life. These prototypes enable you to visualize and test your product's flow without needing extensive coding expertise. It's a valuable step in refining the user experience.

Functional Specifications: The Blueprint for Development

As a founder, it's crucial to communicate your product's intricacies effectively, whether you plan to develop it yourself or collaborate with technical experts. Functional specifications provide this clarity. Here's what to include:

- **What the feature does:** Offer detailed descriptions of each feature required for your product.
- **Why it's important:** Explain why each feature is vital and how it contributes to the overall UX.
- **How the user interacts with it:** Clarify how users will engage with each feature.

This helps developers understand the intended functionality.

Understanding Technical Aspects: Knowledge Is Power

Even as a nontechnical founder, having a basic understanding of certain technical aspects is empowering. Here are some essentials to consider:

- **Platforms:** Decide whether your product will be a web app, a mobile app, or a combination of both.
- **Integrations:** Consider whether your product needs to connect with other tools or platforms to enhance its functionality.

- **Security:** If your product handles sensitive data, understand the importance of implementing robust security measures.
- **Scalability:** Plan for the future. Consider how your product will accommodate a growing user base or increasing data volume.

Planning the Development: DIY or Hire?

At this point, you'll need to decide whether you're equipped to build your MVP yourself or if you need to bring in technical expertise. I'll empower you with further tech knowledge next and in the resource guide at the end of the book, but sometimes, the complexity of your product might be beyond your immediate capabilities. Here's where you make that critical decision.

Budget and Funding: Turning Vision into Reality

Once you've determined your approach to development, it's time to address the financial side of your venture. You'll need to answer questions such as these:

- **Cost estimation:** Gain a comprehensive understanding of the costs involved in building, marketing, and maintaining your product.
- **Funding options**: If you lack the necessary capital, explore different avenues such as bootstrapping, seeking investors, crowdfunding, or applying for start-up grants.

Testing: Ensuring a Flawless Product

Before the grand unveiling of your product, thorough testing is essential. It ensures that your creation functions as intended and offers a seamless experience. Here's how to approach it:

- **Internal testing:** Begin with an internal round of testing within your team. It's a chance to iron out initial issues and improve the overall functionality.

- **Beta testing:** Consider creating a beta testing group and release your product to a limited audience. Their feedback will provide valuable insights to fine-tune your product.
- **Usability testing:** Ensure that your product is user-friendly through rigorous usability testing. It's about making sure your users can effortlessly navigate and engage with your creation.

Launch and Beyond: Your Product's Journey Begins

When you're confident in your MVP, it's time for the grand launch. But remember, this is just the beginning of your product's journey. Here's what to keep in mind:

- **Launch:** Release your product to your target audience. The moment you've been working toward is finally here.
- **Gather feedback:** Never stop listening to your users. Their insights and feedback are invaluable as you continue to refine and improve your product.
- **Iterate:** The journey doesn't end with the launch. Continuously iterate and enhance your product based on feedback and data. It's how you'll stay relevant and continue to meet your users' evolving needs.

Keep in mind that many successful products were started by nontechnical founders. Your expertise and vision, combined with the right collaborators and tools, can lead to a successful product. This chapter aims to equip you with the knowledge, tools, and confidence to take that first step toward building your tech-enabled future.

■ ■ ■

Before we dive into the world of coding, I want you to take a moment to acknowledge the tremendous progress you've made. You've transformed an idea into a comprehensive plan for your MVP product build, and that's no small feat. It's a testament to your dedication and determination. In this next section, my aim is to equip you with the invaluable knowledge of thinking like a coder, a skill that will serve you well whether you're building the product yourself or guiding a team through the process.

How to Think Like a Coder

Coding isn't just about deciphering lines of complex symbols on a computer screen; it's a unique way of thinking and problem-solving. Picture it like this: what if you could don a pair of special glasses that allowed you to view the world through the eyes of a coder? How would your perspective change? The shift would be profound. Let's explore this coding mindset.

- **Break big problems into smaller ones:** Consider a massive puzzle. Attempting to solve it all at once can be daunting. However, if you break it into smaller, manageable sections, suddenly, the challenge becomes much more achievable. This is precisely how coders approach complex issues. When faced with a problem, they break it down into smaller components and methodically address each one.

    Action tip: Apply this approach to your business endeavors. Rather than contemplating the entire project at once, dissect it into individual features or components. This makes problem-solving more manageable.

- **Think logically and then flow:** Have you ever played the game "If this, then that"? One action hinges on another. For instance, "If it's raining, then take an umbrella." Coders use this type of thinking extensively. They build programs based on conditions, ensuring that everything flows in the correct sequence.

Action tip: In your decision-making processes, always consider the cause-and-effect relationship. If you make a particular choice, what will be the outcome? This aids in anticipating challenges and proactively finding solutions.

- **Embrace mistakes:** Surprisingly, coders make mistakes regularly. However, they don't view these errors as failures; instead, they see them as valuable clues. Each mistake illuminates what doesn't work, guiding them closer to a solution.

  Action tip: In the realm of business, don't dread mistakes. Embrace them as learning opportunities. Every misstep is a chance for improvement and innovation.

- **Be patient and persistent:** Coding demands patience. Sometimes, the solution isn't immediately apparent. Coders understand that they may need to explore multiple approaches before uncovering the correct one. They persevere, refusing to give up easily.

  Action tip: When confronted with obstacles in your business journey, don't be disheartened. Maintain your determination and explore various avenues until you discover the most suitable solution.

- **Use the power of computational thinking:** Though it may sound sophisticated, computational thinking is rather straightforward. It involves recognizing patterns, organizing data, and making logical decisions. Think of it as becoming a detective for problems! By adopting this thinking style, you can identify solutions more efficiently and make informed choices.

  Action tip: Always be on the lookout for patterns in your business operations. Perhaps your customers consistently pose the same questions, or a particular product experiences heightened demand during specific seasons. Recognizing these patterns equips you to adapt and thrive.

The Four Main Tools (or Steps) of Computational Thinking

Thinking like a coder doesn't necessitate becoming a computer expert. It's about embracing a problem-solving approach that proves valuable in various aspects of life, particularly in business. I've personally found that this coding-inspired way of thinking has not only assisted me in building a company but also in tackling new challenges, even in something as unrelated as running. By dissecting problems, thinking logically, learning from blunders, maintaining persistence, and identifying patterns, you'll possess a toolbox to confront any obstacle that crosses your path.

The concept of computational thinking, the foundation of computer science, underpins all these principles. Let's delve deeper into it.

Imagine your brain as a toy toolbox. Computational thinking is akin to selecting specific tools from that box to solve problems, much like a builder chooses tools to construct a house.

- **Decomposition:** Imagine you have a massive puzzle. What do you do first? You might sort the pieces by color or start with the edge pieces. That's decomposition—breaking a problem into smaller, more manageable parts.
- **Pattern recognition:** Think about finding a matching pair of socks. You look for socks with the same color or pattern. This is pattern recognition—identifying similarities or trends in data.
- **Abstraction:** Imagine you're drawing a simple picture of the sun. You don't need to include every tiny detail; you focus on the essentials, like a circle with some rays. That's abstraction—concentrating on the crucial information and ignoring the rest.
- **Algorithm design:** Now, picture learning a new dance. You need to know the sequence of steps, which foot moves first, second, and so on. This is algorithm design—creating a step-by-step plan to solve a problem.

Applying Computational Thinking to Building a Product

Let's bring computational thinking to life by using the example of creating a digital lemonade stand.

- **Decomposition:** We break down our lemonade stand idea into manageable parts:
  o Design our stand.
  o Set a price for our lemonade.
  o Advertise to potential customers.
- **Pattern recognition:** We notice that many successful lemonade stands use bright colors and play fun music. Recognizing these patterns can guide our strategy for success!
- **Abstraction:** Rather than getting bogged down in every tiny detail, such as the number of ice cubes in each glass, we focus on significant aspects, like ensuring our "Buy Now" button is prominently visible to customers.
- **Algorithm design:** We formulate a plan:
  o Open the lemonade stand app.
  o Choose the type of lemonade to offer.
  o Set the price.
  o Share our stand with friends and family to attract customers.

Now, even if you're not the one writing the code, comprehending these steps holds immense value:

- If you opt for a no-code solution, you'll understand how to arrange blocks or steps in platforms like Wix or Zapier, much like we planned our digital lemonade stand.
- If you wish to employ automations, you can do so by grasping the sequence of steps (algorithm). This knowledge enables you to set up automated tasks in applications like Google Sheets or MailChimp, such as sending a thank-you email every time someone purchases your lemonade. Remember, computational thinking is like a set of tools in

your mental toolbox. With these tools, you can craft, strategize, and solve problems, even if you never write a single line of code!

Maybe I've now convinced you of the power of learning to code and the value that thinking like a coder can bring to building for the future. If so, you might be asking yourself how to choose the right coding language and how to get started. Let's dive in.

Choosing the right coding language is a decision worth pondering before diving in. Unfortunately, you can't use an app like Duolingo to learn this type of language, but fear not: there are easy tools at your disposal. When I was grappling with the decision of where to begin, part of my choice was influenced by my graduate school coursework, which was centered on Java. However, as I ventured into the start-up realm, I sought a language better suited for interaction and rapid development. For me, that language was Ruby. I relished the ability to tap into Ruby Gems and avoid building everything from the ground up. Speed was of the essence; I wanted to swiftly transform my vision into reality through my product. I noticed that many start-ups, even in their early days, favored Ruby, and this reinforced my choice.

Another factor to consider is whether you have team members who already possess coding knowledge. What languages are they familiar with? Are you collaborating or planning to collaborate with a development team? What language do they primarily use? Although the fundamentals of coding remain consistent across languages, each has its own unique syntax and idiosyncrasies, so choose judiciously. Here are some of the top choices I've observed start-ups gravitating toward when learning to code:

- **Scratch:** This beginner-friendly tool enables you to drag and drop blocks, similar to playing with LEGO, to issue instructions. It's perfect for crafting animations and games, making it an excellent starting point.

- **Python:** Picture a versatile toy that's easy for kids to play with but also packs advanced features for older kids. That's Python. It's beginner-friendly yet powerful enough for substantial projects, making it well suited for web apps, data science, and more.
- **JavaScript:** Think of JavaScript as the magic wand for websites. With it, you can infuse websites with interactivity, such as making a button change color when clicked.
- **HTML/CSS:** In the vast book of the internet, HTML forms the words, while CSS provides the decoration. These are fundamental for web design and structure.
- **Swift:** If you're passionate about Apple products and dream of creating apps for iPhones and iPads, Swift is your go-to language.
- **Ruby:** Imagine Ruby as a magical chest brimming with sparkling gems. Each gem (a software package) can empower your code with special abilities without the need to create everything from scratch. It's particularly fantastic for building web applications, especially when paired with the Rails framework. Ruby is beloved for its elegance and the plethora of gems that expedite coding while making it more enjoyable.
- **No-code:** Although not a traditional coding language, there are remarkable no-code platforms such as Bubble. Depending on the speed at which you require specific features and scalability, these platforms could be the ideal solution.

So, how do you decide which one to use?
First, consider what you want to build:

- For animated stories or beginner games, Scratch is an excellent choice.
- If you're aiming to create websites, dive into HTML/CSS and JavaScript. If you aspire to craft powerful web apps

with the magic of gems, Ruby, especially with Rails, is a fantastic option.

- If your goal is to develop mobile apps for Apple devices, Swift is the path to follow.

Next, evaluate your comfort level:

- If you're entirely new to coding and seek a super-friendly starting point, Scratch is your best bet.
- If you're comfortable with some typing and want versatility to build various things, Python is a great choice.
- If you adore elegant code and the idea of enhancing your projects with ready-to-use gems, dive headfirst into Ruby.

Remember, each coding language and tool possesses its own magic. Ruby Gems, in particular, can save you significant time and enable you to incorporate remarkable features into your projects. The world of coding is expansive and beautiful—find your favorite corner and commence building!

Now that you've determined which coding language you want to use, let me shine a light on a few other coding areas that hold immense value for founders.

Coding Concepts

In the realm of computer science, there are several concepts that I believe are vital to comprehend, even if you don't plan to write lines of code yourself. This understanding profoundly influences the product development process. One concept I've found particularly valuable is object-oriented programming (OOP). My grasp of this concept enabled me to collaborate closely with our engineering team when we developed the next iteration of our product beyond the MVP. This understanding smoothed out the development process considerably. Allow me to walk you through this concept using our digital lemonade stand as an example.

Imagine a Digital Lemonade Stand

Think of it as a computer game where you operate your very own lemonade stand. In this game, various elements come into play:

- **The lemonade stand itself:** This is where you sell lemonade.
- **The lemons:** You use them to make lemonade.
- **The cups:** Customers need these to drink lemonade.
- **The customers:** They come and buy lemonade from you.

In the world of computer programming, each of these elements can be considered as a special box or container. Inside each box, you'll find characteristics and actions related exclusively to that item. For instance, inside the lemonade stand box, you might find details like its location or the price of a cup of lemonade. Similarly, in the customer box, you could find attributes like the customer's name or the amount of money they have.

These boxes, along with their specific details and actions, are what we refer to as objects in OOP. So, when we talk about OOP, we are essentially discussing a way of structuring our program using these objects, where each object represents a unique entity with its own attributes and behaviors.

Objects and Their Properties

Let's delve a bit deeper so you can see it applied clearer to the lemonade stand example.

- **The lemonade stand:**

Properties: color, size, location
Actions: Open the stand, close the stand, sell lemonade.

- **The lemons:**

Properties: size, color, freshness
Actions: Squeeze to get juice, throw away if bad.

■ **The cups:**

Properties: material (plastic, paper), size (small, large)
Actions: Fill with lemonade, give to a customer.

■ **The customers:**

Properties: age, favorite flavor (plain, with mint)
Actions: Walk to the stand, buy lemonade, drink lemonade.

■ **Each box or object:**

Properties: These are akin to descriptions, for example, the color of the lemon.

Actions: Things it can do, such as squeezing a lemon to get juice.

OOP is valuable for building products. Consider if you wanted to modify something or introduce a new feature to your digital lemonade stand game, such as adding a new flavor like strawberry lemonade. If you'd organize everything using objects, it becomes easier! You would merely create a new object for strawberries with its properties (such as color and taste) and actions (mix with lemonade). You wouldn't have to upheave everything else you've already constructed.

When building your MVP, employing OOP offers several advantages:

■ **Organized:** It keeps everything neat and comprehensible.
■ **Flexible:** It simplifies the process of altering, adding, or removing elements without breaking the entire structure.
■ **Reusable:** Should you ever want to develop a new game, such as an ice cream stand, you can recycle some of the components (objects) you initially crafted for the lemonade stand!

This is how we use objects in computer programming to enhance our work and simplify our lives! As you continually iterate on your MVP and monitor your metrics, you'll likely want to make adjustments to the product. Having initially considered the product with OOP in mind will significantly ease this process. I share this because, when I started constructing my MVP, I didn't emphasize OOP as much, and we had to discard certain sections of our code entirely because they didn't facilitate rapid iteration, which is pivotal in the early stages of a product.

The Power of Automation

The power of automation transcends mere time savings for a business. It extends to providing a robust customer service experience, maintaining consistent tracking and reporting, enabling small teams to operate effectively for longer durations, and ultimately saving money while facilitating scalability. I have personally witnessed the tremendous impact automation can have on a business through its implementation in my own company and by assisting hundreds of other companies in this endeavor. Automation empowers your start-up to present itself as more substantial and organized than it might actually be during those early stages of business. In these crucial times, you cannot afford to lose customers due to a high churn rate. Although you may find yourself juggling numerous responsibilities as the founder, often wearing all the hats, automation can provide much-needed support. You might not have the financial means to hire a dedicated customer service team, but you can leverage automation to assemble a makeshift team and grant yourself a few hours of respite before needing to intervene.

I'll continue using the digital lemonade stand as an analogy to illustrate how you can effectively employ automation in your start-up. Allow me to delve further into my affection for automation and its extraordinary potential.

Making Your Start-Up Appear Larger with Automation

Consider a scenario where every time a customer orders a lemonade at your stand, a bell chimes, a thank-you note is dispatched, and the sale is logged—all without your direct involvement. Sounds like magic, doesn't it? Welcome to the realm of automation!

There are so many benefits for start-ups when it comes to automation, but here are the top two that win out:

- **Appear bigger than you are:** Automated systems create the impression of a larger, more organized company. When customers receive instantaneous responses or observe efficient systems in operation, they're more likely to trust your start-up.
- **Reduced 24/7 workload:** As a start-up founder, you wear many hats. Automation enables you to set some of these hats aside, ensuring that tasks are completed while you focus on more substantial challenges (or simply get some well-deserved rest!).

My Favorite Automation Tool: The Magic of Zapier

There are so many automation tools out there today but my favorite and what I feel is the most robust but also easiest to learn is Zapier. Zapier functions like a digital handyman, connecting your tools and orchestrating their seamless collaboration. It can appear to be a bit overwhelming at first if you do not go in with a plan of action. This is because Zapier now has grown to incorporate just about every tool and platform out there, and so you need to know why you want to use it. I am going to break down how I go about using Zapier here. This is a tool that I have worked with hundreds of businesses on to save them hours each week. Here's how you can begin:

- **Identify repetitive tasks:** Before diving into automation, take a week to catalog tasks you repeatedly perform. These might include sending welcome emails to new sign-ups, updating spreadsheets, or following up on inquiries.
- **Start with drag and drop:** Zapier's intuitive interface enables you to link apps and establish workflows using simple drag-and-drop actions. For example, whenever a new user signs up on your website (trigger), you can automatically add them to your email list (action) without lifting a finger.
- **Enhance with code:** If you're comfortable with coding or have access to someone who is, Zapier permits more personalized automations. This means you can fine-tune your workflows to align more precisely with your start-up's requirements. For instance, you can send customized emails based on user behavior or incorporate intricate logic into your workflow. With a bit of code, Zapier can manage it. You can even ask ChatGPT for help with coding these flows.

Automation, particularly in the early stages of a start-up, goes beyond mere efficiency; it plays a pivotal role in shaping your brand's image and ensuring consistent customer experiences. Zapier serves as a bridge between your tools, ensuring they communicate seamlessly without requiring manual intervention. Beginning is as straightforward as pinpointing repetitive tasks and employing drag-and-drop methods, but the platform's potential for customization through code makes it scalable as your start-up expands.

Keep in mind, in the start-up realm, time is a precious commodity. Every second saved through automation is time better spent on innovation, strategy, and, occasionally, well-deserved relaxation. Embrace the enchantment of automation and allow your start-up to shine brilliantly!

Founders frequently inquire about other areas of automation beyond customer service, and although I could write an entire book on this topic, I'd like to share the primary areas where automation can make a profound impact on your start-up. These insights should get you started and excited about incorporating automation into your business, freeing up your time to focus on revenue-generating activities. Here are the top areas:

- **Lead management:** Automate the collection and organization of leads from various sources (e.g., website sign-ups, social media inquiries). Ensure they flow seamlessly into your customer relationship management program or email list and even trigger automated follow-up emails.
- **Customer onboarding:** When someone becomes a customer or subscriber, automation tools can guide them through the process. This includes welcome emails, set-up guides, or even personalized product recommendations based on their preferences.
- **Invoicing and payments:** Automatically send invoices to clients after purchases or subscriptions. Set reminders for unpaid bills and even automate follow-ups for late payments.
- **Social media and content posting:** Schedule and post content across various platforms without manual intervention. These tools can also automate content recycling by reposting evergreen content (informative and relevant material that remains useful to readers regardless of when it is accessed) at set intervals.
- **Inventory and order management:** If you sell physical goods, automation can monitor inventory levels and even initiate restocking orders. For digital products or services, automate the delivery of access or download links on purchase.
- **Feedback and reviews:** After delivering a product or service, automate requests for feedback or reminders to leave

reviews for customers. This continuous feedback can be invaluable for product improvement.

- **Data backups and syncing:** Automate regular backups of crucial data to ensure preparedness for unforeseen issues. Additionally, sync data across different platforms to always have up-to-date information.
- **Task assignments:** Particularly useful in team settings, automation can assign tasks based on specific triggers. For example, if a customer support ticket comes in, it can be automatically assigned to available team members on a rotational basis.
- **Analytics and reporting:** Rather than manually extracting data, automate the generation of weekly or monthly reports on business-critical metrics, such as website traffic, sales conversions, and social media engagement.
- **Customer support:** Use chatbots to handle common inquiries 24/7. Although they can't entirely replace the human touch, they can manage basic queries and direct more complex issues to your human team.

By automating these areas within your start-up, you not only streamline operations but also ensure consistency in processes. This consistent, efficient approach can enhance the user experience, reduce errors, and free up your time to focus on scaling and strategic planning. Remember, the goal isn't to replace the human touch but to complement it with efficient processes.

The Power of Artificial Intelligence

This isn't a book on AI, but it's a book about the incredible value that tech knowledge brings to building a start-up, and the future undeniably involves AI. Therefore, it's crucial to include a section on this topic. I understand that AI is evolving rapidly, and some of the specifics discussed here might become outdated in a short span. Hence, I've opted to focus this section on the over-arching power of tools such as ChatGPT in assisting founders. Whether you're just beginning your coding journey or need specific code segments to aid your automation efforts, ChatGPT and Copilot can be invaluable allies.

Imagine having a friend who's a puzzle wizard. You're staring at a complex jigsaw puzzle, unsure of where to begin, and this friend softly whispers hints and guidance in your ear. ChatGPT (for general advice) and Copilot (for coding assistance) are akin to these helpful whispering friends. Here's how to make the most of them:

- **Start with an idea:** First and foremost, have a clear vision of what you want to build. It could be as simple as a website showcasing your favorite recipes or as complex as an app reminding you to stay hydrated.
- **Seek general guidance from ChatGPT:** If you're uncertain about where to commence, describe your idea to ChatGPT just as you would to a friend. For instance, "I'd like to create a straightforward website for my recipes." ChatGPT can provide general advice, suggest appropriate tools, or even recommend coding languages that align with your project.
- **Delve into coding with Copilot:** Once you've identified a direction, Copilot becomes your trusty copilot throughout the coding journey. Even if your coding knowledge is limited to statements like "I want a button here," Copilot can assist in transforming that concept into actual code by offering suggestions on how that button's code might appear.
- **Employ prompts and questions:** These tools excel in their interactivity; you can pose questions! For instance, "How can I make this button red?" or "I'd like the website's background to feature a sunset image." The more precise your inquiries, the more accurate the suggestions you'll receive.

- **Practice and learn:** As you rely on Copilot and ChatGPT, you'll gradually discern recurring patterns in the code. With time, your dependence on asking for guidance will decrease, and you'll become more adept at taking action. These tools not only help you complete tasks but also serve as educators in their own right.
- **Debugging and troubleshooting:** Encountering an error? Describe the issue. Frequently, these tools can propose solutions or direct you to resources where you might find the answers you seek.

You don't need to be a coding virtuoso to begin. Tools like ChatGPT and Copilot provide real-time assistance and guidance. They aren't just about furnishing answers; over time, you'll develop a deeper understanding of the why behind coding solutions. Although these tools are formidable, remember to supplement your learning with other resources and tutorials. A multipronged approach will enrich your comprehension.

So, take that intricate coding puzzle and dive in! With these supportive whisperers accompanying you on the journey, you're never alone.

Code Review: Crafting Your Tech Founder Toolbox

Much like an experienced coder scrutinizes their code for optimization, as a prospective tech-savvy founder, you must assess which technological components will empower your start-up journey most effectively. In this code review, we'll dissect the four core pillars of tech prowess—coding, computational thinking, automation, and AI—and determine which ones align most harmoniously with your start-up's vision. Furthermore, we'll revisit your product planning to ensure it's fortified with the insights you've gained.

Let's delve into this code review for crafting your tech founder toolbox:

- **Coding:** Reflect on your current coding knowledge and its relevance to your start-up. Do you see yourself taking a hands-on approach to code your product, or would you prefer a foundational understanding to communicate effectively with your tech team?
- **Computational thinking:** Assess the degree to which you've incorporated computational thinking into your product planning. Have you adeptly broken down complex problems into smaller, manageable components? Is logical flow evident in your product's development road map?
- **Automation:** Evaluate your start-up's potential for automation. How can it save time, enhance customer service, or streamline operations? Are there specific areas, such as lead management or customer support, where automation could be a game-changer for your venture?
- **AI:** Contemplate the role of AI in your start-up. Could it elevate customer experiences, provide data-driven insights, or automate decision-making processes? Determine if integrating AI aligns with your long-term vision.
- **Balancing act:** Strive for balance. Which combination of these tech components—coding, computational thinking, automation, or AI—resonates most with your start-up's needs?
- **Product planning check-in:** Revisit your product planning with fresh insights gained during this journey. How can your newfound tech wisdom augment your product's road map? Are there areas where you can incorporate computational thinking or automation more strategically?
- **Iterative progress:** Remember, the journey of a tech-savvy founder is iterative, much like refining a complex code

base. The flexibility to adapt and integrate technology seamlessly into your start-up's fabric will set you on a path to innovation and transformative impact.

Embrace this code review as a pivotal moment in your tech founder quest. Your ability to discern and incorporate the most suitable tech elements is the key to building a start-up that thrives in the digital age.

PART

III

Building Together

10

The GAPS

Data, Care, and Funding

There were five exabytes of information created between the dawn of civilization through 2003, but that much information is now created every two days.

—Eric Schmidt, executive chairman at Google

I want every woman to unashamedly set out to make an absolute goddamn f*cking sh*t-ton of money. Because when we make an absolute goddamn f*cking sh*t-ton of money, we can use that money to fund other women. Help other women. Support other women. Donate to other women. We need to build our own financial and business ecosystem because the white male one isn't working for us. That's why I tell women, "Start your own industry."

—Cindy Gallop, equal rights activist and founder of MakeLoveNotPorn

THERE ARE TIMES when your code is not complete when writing a program. There might be gaps or missing symbols or parts of the language when coding that keep it from compiling correctly. Just as with coding in the real world, there are gaps that affect the

145

building and success of start-ups. That is what we will dive into in this chapter. When I embarked on my journey as a founder, I had the potent combination of naivety and optimism on my side. Back then, my limited knowledge of the intricacies of entrepreneurship was a blessing. It enabled me to operate with unwavering passion and enthusiasm, unburdened by the vast complexities that lay ahead. Sure, I knew it wouldn't be easy; I'd heard the statistics that most start-ups fail. However, the real challenges and gaps that women face while building a business only became apparent as my own venture grew.

Looking back now, I realize that my initial naivety might have been a double-edged sword. It postponed my confrontation with the harsh realities that women in entrepreneurship often grapple with. These gaps, these disparities in data, care, and funding, eventually caught up with me. If I could turn back time, I'd want to confront them head on much earlier in my journey. In this chapter I share my and other founders' experiences with these challenges because I believe that we need to face them head on together.

The Gender Data Gap

For me, knowledge is power. I thrive on data, information, and informed decision-making. The lack of this crucial data in the world of female entrepreneurship troubled me deeply. Our stories, struggles, and achievements weren't being adequately recorded. The information gap was glaring, and this was one of the driving forces behind me writing this book. I felt that there should be a comprehensive resource for women in entrepreneurship, a repository of knowledge and stories that can help bridge these gaps.

I'd like to take a moment to recommend a book that delves into this issue in a profound way—*Invisible Women: Data Bias in a World Designed for Men* by Caroline Criado Perez. Reading it was certainly an eye-opener for me.

The book reveals the pervasive bias embedded in systems that many take for granted as neutral. This isn't a mere matter of overt sexism; it's subtler, more concealed. It's the systematic omission of women from foundational data that informs everything from urban planning to the algorithms running our digital world.

The implications stretch across numerous fields. Consider urban planning: cities and transportation, often viewed through a gender-neutral lens, repeatedly neglect the distinct needs of women, who, due to societal roles and expectations, might navigate urban environments differently.

Medical research offers another stark example. The disproportionate focus on male subjects means there's a gaping hole in our understanding of how treatments affect women, leading to significant health disparities.

The technology sector is particularly vulnerable to these biases. When products or digital tools are designed primarily with male users in mind, they can become not just inconvenient but also less effective for women. AI and large language models (LLMs), which are at the forefront of technological advancements, are no exception. If these models are trained on data dominated by male perspectives or on historical texts that reflect male-centric views, they perpetuate and amplify existing biases. For instance, an AI system can offer skewed outputs or an LLM might generate content that subtly supports or magnifies male-centric worldviews.

Criado Perez masterfully combines data, sharp analysis, and compelling narratives to spotlight these systemic gaps. The message of *Invisible Women* isn't just about identifying the problem— it's a rallying cry for change. As we continue to advance into a data-driven era, especially in AI development, we must critically assess which data we prioritize and ensure that we're capturing the full spectrum of human experience, not just half of it.

In history classes and discussions about wartime, we primarily focus on the war itself, its strategies, and the men who fought it.

Rarely do we delve into the experiences of those who were not at the frontline but were heavily affected by it—women. Take World War II, for example. Although we might know about Rosie the Riveter and the contribution of women in factories, lesser known are the stories of women who received government-supported childcare during that time to facilitate their employment. These stories were often left untold until recently.

A perfect illustration of these sidelined narratives is the story of the ENIAC, the electronic numerical integrator and computer. Although ENIAC is lauded as the world's first general-purpose electronic digital computer, what's often glossed over is the instrumental role played by six incredible women during its inception. These were not just any contributors; they were the primary programmers: Jean Jennings Bartik, Frances "Betty" Snyder Holberton, Kathleen "Kay" McNulty Mauchly Antonelli, Marlyn Wescoff Meltzer, Ruth Lichterman Teitelbaum, and Frances Bilas Spence.

Without the luxury of a programming manual or a road map, these women innovatively tackled the ENIAC's challenges. They deduced its operations, creating foundational techniques that would set the stage for software programming's future. Beyond its intended artillery calculations, they ventured into realms of weather prediction, atomic energy computations, and even feasibility studies for the hydrogen bomb.

Yet, despite the enormity of their contributions, they remained unsung heroes for the longest time. Their achievements were eclipsed by a male-dominated narrative, leaving them relegated to the annals of forgotten history. It was only when a persistent researcher, driven by a sense of historical justice, unearthed their story that the world began to recognize their true worth.

Their legacy serves as a potent reminder: women have always been at the forefront of technological and innovative breakthroughs. As we gaze toward the future, let's continue to champion the incredible women who shape and redefine our world.

How Can We Bridge This Data Gap?

It's a colossal challenge, but one that we can certainly tackle. When I first delved into the intricacies of the data gap, it was like opening a door to a new reality. As someone with a background in history and life experience as a woman and mother, I had an inkling that this gap existed, but it wasn't until I read *Invisible Women* that I was confronted with the staggering scope of the issue. This void in data, especially in the era of AI where data reigns supreme, demanded a solution. Here's what I've gathered on how we can begin to address this massive problem:

- **Awareness and advocacy:** The first step to fixing any problem is recognizing its existence. Use every platform available, in the physical and digital realms, to raise awareness about the data gap. Engage stakeholders in dialogues that elucidate why closing this gap is vital for building a fair and equitable society. It's time for this issue to take center stage from conference halls to boardrooms and workplaces.

- **Diverse data collection teams:** To truly understand and rectify data gaps and biases, it's essential to have diverse teams collecting data. Teams composed of individuals from various genders, ethnicities, and backgrounds are more likely to detect these gaps and ensure that data collection methods are comprehensive and inclusive. Next time you're asked to provide data, consider who's collecting it and how they're doing it.

- **Inclusion in decision-making:** Whether we're discussing disaster recovery strategies or shaping the next breakthrough in technology, women must have a seat at the decision-making table. Their unique perspectives can fill gaps that might otherwise remain unnoticed.

- **Collaborative historical research:** Encourage and fund research projects that aim to uncover forgotten contributions, particularly those made by women. These projects can take a collaborative approach, drawing from oral histories, archived documents, and other invaluable sources.

- **Mandatory gender data reporting:** Encourage organizations, especially in the tech and AI sectors, to provide regular reports on gender-related statistics and be transparent about their efforts to address any gender disparities.
- **Education and curriculum reform:** We must integrate stories of women's remarkable contributions into mainstream educational curricula. This ensures that future generations grow up knowing about these invaluable contributions.
- **Develop gender-sensitive AI tools:** Given the increasing influence of AI in decision-making, it's crucial to invest in tools capable of detecting and correcting gender biases within datasets.
- **Safe reporting mechanisms:** In contexts such as natural disasters and wartime, establish mechanisms that enable women to safely report their needs, concerns, and experiences.
- **Women-focused technology grants:** Financially support tech projects and start-ups that aim to tackle women-specific issues or are led by women, fostering a more balanced tech landscape.
- **Mentorship and networking:** Successful women in tech and other fields should step up as mentors for younger women and provide networking opportunities. This creates a supportive ecosystem where women can thrive and ensures their contributions aren't overlooked. Document these initiatives and make sure they're shared company- or organization-wide.
- **Digital archiving:** Employ digital platforms to archive and showcase women's contributions. Platforms such as Wikipedia, for instance, play a pivotal role in modern knowledge dissemination. Ensuring a strong presence there guarantees that women's stories are not only told but easily accessible.

- **Community engagement:** Engage with communities to gain a deeper understanding of women's experiences. This grassroots approach ensures that solutions are tailored to real needs, rather than being based on assumptions.

Closing the gender data gap isn't just about gathering more data about women; it's about using data to craft inclusive and effective solutions. This demands systemic change, a reimagining of how we approach data collection, analysis, and implementation. It begins with recognizing and valuing the contributions of women, both historically and in contemporary times. It's a collective effort, and by acknowledging these gaps, we can begin to bridge them, one step at a time.

Pause and Reflect

The gender care gap isn't just a statistic; it's a lived experience for many. Instead of doing a full code review at the end of this chapter for each gap area, I wanted to do a shorter reflection at the end of each one. Before we move on, let's take a moment to internalize these insights and consider their broader implications. Use the following questions to deepen your understanding and connection to this topic:

- **Reflection on current awareness:** Were you previously aware of the gender data gap? How does this newfound understanding align with your personal experiences or observations? How might gender data biases be perpetuated or magnified by AI algorithms? What are the implications if these biases go unchecked in our increasingly digital world?
- **Personal and professional impact on AI and technology:** Can you identify areas in your life or work where you might be using data or tools influenced by gender biases? How could you address this?

- **Championing diversity in data collection:** How can organizations ensure that their data collection is inclusive, capturing diverse perspectives beyond just gender, such as race, age, and socioeconomic status?
- **Challenging the status quo and collaborative efforts:** How do societal norms and traditional roles contribute to the gender data gap, and how can collaboration among stakeholders lead to equitable data practices?
- **Personal action and accountability:** What steps can you take in the near future to contribute to addressing the gender data gap within your sphere of influence?

The Care Gap

In March 2020, I was in New York City for an event for the Female Founders Collective, and little did I know what the world had in store with the impending COVID-19 pandemic. We were just starting to hear murmurs about it, and I was already armed with hand sanitizers and wipes. Fate had it that I was staying at the same hotel as Blessing Adesiyan, the remarkable founder of MH Work-Life. We ended up spending more time together at the event due to our hotel proximity, and I'm profoundly grateful for that. It was a time when the world was still buzzing with energy and optimism. Looking back, it serves as a reminder of women's unwavering determination. We might slow down momentarily, but we never stop moving toward our vision because we're building not just for ourselves but for humanity. Blessing's mission was to build a future of better care for all. She recognized that for women to thrive in their entrepreneurial journeys we need robust care structures and support integrated into our work environments. Specifically, these are systems that address the challenges of balancing work with caregiving responsibilities, making it easier for women to manage their professional aspirations and their roles as primary caregivers.

This care gap, emblematic of the rigid constraints of traditional workplaces, drove me to leave my regular job in favor of freelancing. This lack of flexibility and support was a contributing factor for the more than two million women who exited the workforce during the pandemic and explains why an alarming 43% of educated women leave their jobs annually (https://www.theatlantic.com/sexes/archive/2013/04/why-43-of-women-with-children-leave-their-jobs-and-how-to-get-them-back/275134/).

Early in 2020, we were gearing up to launch Allobee out of closed beta. Then, the world stopped. My kids were home from school, childcare options evaporated, and we were confined to our homes. Those few weeks in March forced me into some soul-searching conversations with myself and our small team. We were still in our infancy, and the future looked uncertain, but it was also a period that granted us the flexibility to adapt. We postponed our launch from March to May. We pivoted from being a marketplace of goods and services to focusing solely on freelance services. I had a mere three weeks to overhaul our minimum viable product (MVP) to meet our new public launch deadline. It was an intense time. I had my kids at home, and my husband was working full-time. To this day, I'm not entirely sure how I managed it, except for the unwavering support of my husband and the principles we embraced from Eve Rodsky's *Fair Play* book. This method helped us distribute household responsibilities and navigate through the pandemic. We were fortunate that our kids returned to in-person school in fall 2020. If they hadn't, I'm not sure if Allobee would have survived. The broken state of childcare in our country primarily affects women, and the pandemic intensified this issue. In fall 2020, I spent my days fundraising. I couldn't have done that with the kids at home.

The Care Gap Interviews

On my podcast, *Allobee Radio*, I have had the privilege of interviewing several entrepreneurs about their experiences during 2020. Their insights during those challenging times left a lasting impact and really hit on areas of the care gap. Let me share excerpts from two of these conversations:

Reshma Saujani
Founder of Girls Who Code and CEO of MOMS F1RST

The Future of Work for Moms Summit, May 2020

I have admired Reshma and the advocacy she has brought through her career to support girls, women, and moms. She has fought to get us better access, education, and support structures. When she said yes to being one of our fireside chat speakers for our summit that launched my company, I was so honored.

Brooke: I would like to ask you about the fundamental changes needed in our society to create a positive future of work for mothers. Do you find this to be an exhausting challenge?

Reshma: Structurally, there's a definite need for more flexibility. Personally, as a CEO, I can set my own hours. For me, being able to wake up in the morning, get my son ready for school, take him to school, and then do something for myself before heading to work is incredible. It's about not feeling like I'm making a choice, but rather integrating everything. For instance, if I've been traveling for a few days and I want to drop by my son's music class, I can do that. I encourage all the women in my office to do the same. The powerful lesson here is that women can be mothers and be highly productive at work; it's not an either-or situation. We should encourage more mothers and women to work from home because there's something beautiful about having your kids nearby. You miss them when you're away. There's a unique comfort in that. The second thing we need to change, and it's not our fault, is this idea that we have to prove we can do both perfectly. We need to stop pretending we can do everything. That means we have to stop hiding the fact that we're mothers. Many young women in their 20s and 30s who work with me are concerned about their careers when they don't even have children yet. I remind them not to worry about it. When I had my first child, I intentionally brought him everywhere with me. I wanted to show that it's okay to be a messy leader with your kids. It's okay for it to be chaotic. It's fine if your outfit gets ruined. We must accept that it's part of the journey. One of the valuable lessons I've learned is that it's fine to have your kids around while doing everything—having dinner, watching a movie, even when you want to unwind with a glass of wine—they're there, everywhere. We've learned that it's alright; you don't have to choose. But not choosing also means embracing imperfection and the messiness of life.

Pamela Pekerman
Founder of Hustle Like A Mom
Allobee Radio, Episode 54

Moms that live the life of the "drop-off to pick-up entrepreneur" have a special place in my heart. They are the ones I fully understand. I have been there and am still there in many ways. What I learned in this phase of my life was invaluable. One of the best examples of a "drop-off to pick-up entrepreneur" is my friend Pamela Pekerman of Hustle Like A Mom. She is fabulous and a true example of MOMentum. I had the honor of interviewing her during the pandemic, and her insights helped me so much.

Brooke:　Entrepreneurship was my bridge from the tech world, granting me the flexibility I needed for both motherhood and a fulfilling career. Sadly, many women aren't aware of this potential pathway, often because their previous careers didn't expose them to the idea. It's heartening to see women like you advocating for entrepreneurship as a harmonious blend with motherhood. What stories or patterns have you noticed among women in your community who have transitioned into entrepreneurship?

Pamela:　Through my work at "Hustle Like A Mom," I've engaged with a multitude of women who once thrived in traditional careers. Many left due to lack of fulfillment or changing personal circumstances and felt stranded years later, believing it was too late to return to their old profession. The increase in such stories, especially post-2020, shows that women are realizing the opportunities entrepreneurship offers.

　　　　But I'm cautious about glamorizing it. Nadia Murdoch, a fitness expert and a previous PR professional, always emphasized realism. Before leaping into entrepreneurship, review your financial standing and discuss with your life partner about your intentions. If you're fortunate to have a stable job, consider letting it fund your entrepreneurial journey until you're ready to make the transition.

　　　　For women today, there are myriad opportunities. Whether you're crafting jewelry, offering a service, or mastering platforms like Instagram, there's a niche. It's about flexibility. As Julie Cole from Mabel's Labels pointed out, entrepreneurship is deciding which 12-hour shift suits you. It requires periodic reassessment of goals aligned with changing personal circumstances.

Brooke: It's crucial to set realistic expectations. Perfectionists like me often struggle with the gradual nature of entrepreneurial success. While many commend my recent achievements, it's a culmination of six years of persistent effort. And you're absolutely right about the importance of communicating with partners or spouses.

Pamela: Communication isn't just limited to partners. Depending on your child's age, involve them, too. My children are attuned to my work schedule. They recognize when I have podcasts, meetings, or when I'm leading a Zoom session. If you're transitioning into entrepreneurship, it's imperative to communicate the impending lifestyle changes with your family. Assumptions can lead to misunderstandings, and being up front can alleviate that.

Pamela's insights resonate deeply. Effective communication forms the bedrock of a harmonious work-life integration. My initial phase with MOMentum, which later evolved into Allobee, was riddled with communication hiccups. Such experiences have since underlined its importance in ensuring growth and balance. Building as a mom is hard, and the care gap and issues that stem from it are hard to navigate.

Motherhood's Transformative Power

Becoming a mother changes you at a profound level, altering your very essence at the cellular level. Your body undergoes a remarkable transformation to nurture and grow a tiny human, and this transformation extends far beyond the physical. It affects your brain chemistry, your body, and equally your mind and soul. Motherhood was a seismic shift in my life, reshaping the very fabric of my being. I've come to believe that motherhood not only fostered my entrepreneurial spirit but also set it ablaze with a burning desire to construct a better world for my children.

As I embarked on my entrepreneurial journey, it became glaringly evident that the world was not designed to support me as both a caregiver and a builder.

Challenges of the Care Gap

The cost of childcare since my kids were born represents a staggering figure that's difficult to swallow. And this was with two parents fortunate enough to have relatively flexible schedules, enabling us to piece together a more affordable care arrangement. I'm not suggesting that we should reduce the wages of childcare providers; they deserve more, if anything. But I do believe that as a society, we need to explore options like childcare subsidies or create more flexible work opportunities to alleviate this burden.

I, too, made the choice to leave my traditional career for freelancing, seeking greater flexibility as a mom. However, this decision came at a cost—a significant hit to my personal earning potential and potential future prospects. I have had to intentionally work to make sure I was setting my career up for success long term in its own way outside of the traditional career ladder.

For women to fully pursue their careers and entrepreneurial ambitions, flexibility is essential when they decide to have children. Yet, the need for flexibility doesn't end with motherhood; it extends to anyone who becomes a caregiver, such as when caring for aging parents. Care is a universal need, far beyond just childcare. Blessing Adesiyan, mentioned previously, is dedicated to addressing this issue. Her company focuses on creating innovative care solutions to support a resilient and productive workforce, offering personalized work-life tools, expert guidance, and coverage for care gaps. It's time for society to recognize that care is integral to our well-being and that workplaces must adapt to this reality, not only for retention but also for fostering innovation.

According to the Center for American Progress, in 2018, more than half of Americans lived in "childcare deserts," areas where there were more than three children for every licensed childcare slot (https://www.americanprogress.org/article/child-care-crisis-keeping-women-workforce/). The US Department of Health & Human Services considers childcare costing more than 7% of a family's income as unaffordable. However, in many states, the average cost of childcare far exceeds this threshold (https://www.americanprogress.org/article/working-families-spending-big-money-child-care/).

The Care Gap Dimensions

The childcare gap is a multifaceted issue, encompassing several dimensions:

- **Availability:** In many regions, there's a simple lack of childcare services or facilities to meet the demand. This leaves parents, usually mothers, struggling to find appropriate care options while they work or attend to other responsibilities.
- **Affordability:** Even when childcare services are available, they can be prohibitively expensive. This often makes it financially impractical for average-income families to use them. In some cases, the cost of childcare can exceed a person's salary, making it uneconomical to work.
- **Quality:** Not all available childcare is of high quality. There can be vast disparities in the standard of care, educational value, and safety offered by different childcare providers.
- **Flexibility:** Many childcare services operate on rigid schedules, which don't align with the nontraditional or extended working hours that many parents require.

This care gap often leads to one parent, historically the mother, having to reduce working hours, take on lesser roles, or exit the workforce entirely to care for their children. This has long-term implications for career trajectories, earning potentials, and gender equality in the workplace.

As we look ahead, the issue of elder care is looming larger on the horizon. As baby boomers continue to age, the care responsibilities for aging parents will increasingly fall on their children, especially women.

The Need for a Different Approach

What I've learned through my journey is that women cannot operate in the same manner as men when building. If we attempt to do so, we risk burnout and failure, not because we lack determination, intelligence, or strength, but because society has not provided us with an equal playing field. We often bear the brunt of unpaid labor, receive only a fraction of venture funding, and this has a substantial impact. When I first started as an entrepreneur, I thought I needed to attend all the networking events and conferences. I wondered how on earth I could do this once I had children. It seemed impossible. But it required a shift in perspective and strategy.

I focused on building long-lasting relationships, and that decision paid off. My initial naivety was both a superpower and a challenge when I began building Allobee. I hadn't fully comprehended the difficulties of building a business as a mom, especially as the demands of the business grew. Sacrifices were inevitable, but problems escalated when I attempted to ignore the care gap and operate like a man. There is an undeniable gap for women, and it's essential that we don't disregard it, or we risk burnout. We must recognize that women often operate differently, both in terms of their energy and leadership style. Embracing these differences and building accordingly can lead to sustainable success.

After diving into the care gap and understanding its complexities, it's crucial to connect these insights to our personal journey. Let's take a brief pause to contemplate how these stories resonate with us. These reflection questions aim to guide you through that process.

Self-Awareness and Personal Experience
- How do your own experiences with care align or diverge from those discussed in this section?
- Can you recall a specific moment when the care gap personally affected your life or career? How did you navigate it?

Societal Implications
- Based on Reshma's and Pamela's insights, what societal norms about caregiving and work do you see being perpetuated in your community or workplace?
- How does the issue of elder care compound the already existing challenges posed by the childcare gap?

Addressing the Care Gap
- In what ways do you believe society could better support mothers (and caregivers in general) in the workplace?
- Considering the dimensions of the childcare gap (availability, affordability, quality, flexibility), which dimension do you believe needs the most immediate attention in your community? Why?

Entrepreneurship and the Care Gap
- How can entrepreneurship be a solution to the care gap for some women? What challenges might arise from this approach?

Embracing Differences
- What strengths do you believe women bring to the table, especially in leadership roles, that are distinct and valuable?

- How can embracing these differences lead to more sustainable success for women entrepreneurs and professionals?

Action and Advocacy
- What steps can individuals take to advocate for more flexibility and support for caregivers in their workplaces?
- How might you support or mentor another woman or caregiver who is navigating the challenges of the care gap?

The Funding Gap

No one likes to admit to a fundraising setback, but I'll candidly share that I faced one. We weren't able to secure our seed round and opted for an acquisition path instead. Several factors were at play, but one significant issue stood out: the starkly limited funding available for women entrepreneurs.

Reflecting on my journey of raising a pre-seed round and attempting a seed round, I realize that starting the seed round earlier might have been beneficial. However, finding the right balance between traction and timing is challenging. Additionally, I wish I had invested more time in networking with investors throughout my entrepreneurial journey. This is a task that should primarily fall to the founder, because investors at these early stages want to connect with and get to know the person driving the venture. The reality is, we need to talk about these setbacks and the reasons we decide to take an alternative route or shut companies down. Most start-ups fail and it is okay, but we need to talk about it and share our learnings so we can make changes and work to fix the systemic issues that are there.

Recently, I met with a founder whom I had connected with during my Allobee pitch at the Venture Atlanta event in 2022. She asked if I'd consider an advisory role in her start-up. Although I often receive such requests, I can't accept all of them. Nonetheless, I'm always willing to have a call or meeting to assess compatibility. During our hour-long conversation, it was frustrating to learn how the allure and pressure to raise venture capital had hindered her ability to establish a solid, sustainable business. I deeply understand this frustration, given my experiences as a start-up founder and my interactions with hundreds of female founders. The prevailing advice in start-up circles and accelerators is to raise funding if you intend to scale. However, what's not emphasized enough is that less than 2% of venture funding goes to female founders, with even less directed toward women of color (https://techcrunch.com/2023/01/18/women-founded-startups-raised-1–9-of-all-vc-funds-in-2022-a-drop-from-2021/). There are seldom workshops on bootstrapping, and it's tragically underappreciated. Slow, sustainable growth is sometimes viewed negatively, but in retrospect, I see that many companies, including mine, could have thrived with this approach. This particular founder is now contemplating a shift toward a sustainable approach, halting all fundraising efforts and seeking help and support within her network in nonfinancial ways. By turning her focus inward, she hopes to achieve success.

Competing for a Fraction of the Pie

Competing for just 2% of the funding pie has, in my opinion, had the most significant impact on female founders. We've often isolated ourselves, believing we must do so to secure funding. Many of us end up approaching the same few female venture capital firms and angel investors who possess a relatively low percentage of overall capital to deploy. I firmly believe that until we disrupt the venture capital industry, there's no clear path for women in general. It's a time-consuming endeavor that diverts energy away from building your company. If more women collaborated instead of competing, numerous companies could merge, provided we set aside our egos. Women are creating incredible, humanity-focused products, and together, we can build the future.

Strategies to Overcome Funding Barriers

My first piece of advice is not to rush into raising money for your business, especially in the early stages. In fact, I believe there should be more voices discouraging it at this point. Although I acknowledge that some businesses are indeed fundable and could benefit from funding, it's essential to recognize that, historically, access to funding has been a significant challenge for female founders. This is despite numerous studies demonstrating that start-ups led by women often outperform those led by men. Although there was talk for a while about changing tides and improved prospects for female founders, I haven't seen conclusive data supporting this claim. Yes, the number of female venture capitalists has increased, but actual returns will take time. It's important to note that slow and sustainable growth isn't celebrated enough, and the pressure to raise venture capital can detract from building a solid business. There are several benefits from getting all of the documents and pitch prepared even if you do not go the traditional funding route. These can help you secure partnerships, sponsors, and even customers. Here are some strategies that I have found valuable in my own fundraising efforts as well as other founders I have mentored:

- **Educate and advocate:** First and foremost, know your numbers. Familiarize yourself with industry statistics concerning female founders and funding, as well as insights into your competitors in the same space. This knowledge can be a powerful tool when framing your discussions and pitches. Use examples of female-founded businesses that have excelled to demonstrate that investing in female founders is a sound business decision. Confidence in your business and what you're building can inspire others to support you.
- **Networking:** Although many suggest seeking out female investors, remember that there are still very few of them,

and they often face a deluge of pitches from female founders. Instead, focus on the investment thesis of firms or angel investors and aim for warm introductions to them. Attending conferences or pitch events where investors gather can also be beneficial. You don't necessarily have to be the one pitching; you can schedule multiple meetings in one go at events such as Venture Atlanta or similar conferences. Female founder organizations can provide support as well, but do your research to ensure they align with your business's stage and offer actionable support or networking opportunities. Building relationships with men who understand and champion diversity can also open doors to funding opportunities.

- **Preparation:** Invest in understanding how to create an effective pitch. This might involve working with a pitch coach or seeking input from founders or friendly investors from different industries. Pitching is an art that requires iterative refinement. Ensure that you are well prepared for each pitch, articulating the problem your start-up solves, your solution, and the market opportunity with confidence. Be prepared for possible disruptions, such as latecomers or last-minute cancellations.

- **Demonstrate traction:** Highlight the metrics you've been focusing on since the MVP stage. If possible, provide real data points showcasing user engagement and sales. Real-world data can make your pitch much more compelling.

- **Consider alternative funding:** Exploring crowdfunding campaigns, such as Kickstarter, Indiegogo, or iFundWomen, can be a viable option for certain products or services. This approach enables you to raise money directly from customers or supporters while validating your market. Although grants for female founders are limited, they do exist, and you should explore local and national opportunities. Angel investors might not be an alternative to venture capital, but they can be more approachable and mission-driven.

- **Accelerators and incubators for women:** Join programs specifically designed for women, such as the Female Founders Alliance or All Raise. They offer mentorship, resources, and sometimes funding opportunities.

- **Educational opportunities:** Although I've previously discussed the importance of being tech-savvy, having strong technological skills can be immensely valuable when raising funds. The more you can build and demonstrate, the better your chances.

- **Seek feedback:** After a pitch, whether successful or not, ask for feedback. Understand any reservations the investor might have had. This feedback can provide valuable insights for refining your pitch in future opportunities.

- **Leverage technology:** Use platforms such as AngelList, Crunchbase, or Carta to research potential investors, understand their portfolios, and tailor your pitch to align with their interests. You can also use tools like ChatGPT to assist with writing emails to investors or identifying firms relevant to your industry.

- **Transparency:** Address potential concerns up front. If there's an area where your business might appear weak, acknowledge it and provide a strategy for how you plan to address it. Controlling your narrative and taking charge of your weaknesses is crucial.

- **Be persistent:** Rejections are an inherent part of the fundraising journey. Learn from them, refine your approach, and keep moving forward. Also, remember that follow-ups are often necessary; rarely does an investor respond positively to the first email.

These strategies, tailored to female founders, embody universal principles of preparation, perseverance, and adaptability that can benefit any entrepreneur in their funding journey.

Code Review: Evaluating Your Fundraising Strategy

In this chapter, we'll conduct a comprehensive code review of your fundraising strategy because funding is so hard for founders and the preparation that goes into fundraising is valuable whether you raise or not. Similar to reviewing a code base for errors and optimizations, we'll analyze your fundraising approach, identify areas that need improvement, and highlight strong elements. Let's start the review:

- **Debugging your value proposition:** Just as a developer ensures code clarity, reflect on your start-up's value proposition. Is it crystal clear, compelling, and tailored to your target audience? Consider ways to make it more distinct.
- **Analyzing and reframing rejections:** Rejections are part of fundraising, like bugs in code. Think about the feedback from past rejections. How can you transform this feedback into actionable insights to refine your pitch?
- **Evaluating your pitch deck:** A pitch deck is your code for conveying your vision. Review yours. Is it concise, engaging, and aligned with your start-up's mission? Identify areas for improvement and update it based on recent developments.
- **Inspecting your network:** Just as a developer checks dependencies, assess the strength and breadth of your network. Are there untapped connections, potential mentors, or industry experts who can assist your fundraising journey?
- **Decoding market trends:** Similar to keeping code up-to-date with libraries, stay current with market trends in your industry. How can you leverage these trends in your fundraising strategy?

- **Debugging preparation for due diligence:** Ensure all your documents, financials, and metrics are well prepared for due diligence, such as testing your code for bugs. Address any gaps proactively to instill investor confidence.
- **Reviewing your negotiation techniques:** Reflect on past negotiations. Were there moments of unpreparedness? Consider strategies to enhance your negotiation skills. Negotiating is similar to debugging code logic.
- **Debugging your understanding of investor profiles:** Just as understanding user behavior is vital in coding, know your potential investors. Are you targeting those whose interests align with your start-up's goals? Deepen your research.
- **Inspecting communication post-fundraising:** Strong post-fundraising communication is essential, much like maintaining code. Reflect on the quality and frequency of your updates to investors. Clear communication is key.
- **Debugging your emotional resilience:** Fundraising can be emotionally demanding. Reflect on how you manage the highs and lows. What techniques can you employ to enhance your emotional resilience?

By conducting this comprehensive review, you'll pinpoint areas that need debugging and areas where your fundraising strategy shines. Remember that debugging is about refinement. Commit to implementing the necessary changes. Embrace the insights gained and navigate your fundraising journey with renewed clarity and confidence. Similar to a well-optimized code base, a well-honed fundraising strategy can lead to success.

11

Women Building

Stories and Roadblocks

The most common way people give up their power is by thinking they don't have any.

—Alice Walker

No country can ever truly flourish if it stifles the potential of its women and deprives itself of the contributions of half of its citizens.

—Michelle Obama

BUILDING CAN BE one of the loneliest endeavors. The journey is marked by passion, excitement, and occasional isolation. As a female founder, I often felt alone during my early days of building, searching in vain for relatable stories. This chapter aims to fill that void by sharing authentic narratives of women who have embarked on similar journeys. Their stories offer invaluable insights into the challenges and triumphs of building.

The absence of these stories is not just a matter of missing data; it's about the absence of shared experiences. The scarcity of women's narratives in entrepreneurship affect our collective understanding and influences decisions. To address this gap, this chapter features more than 40 women's accounts of building. It aims to provide you with a comprehensive view of women shaping the future and reminds you that you're never alone on this journey.

At a Glance: The Numbers

Before diving into their stories, it's important to understand some key statistics that come from the She's Next Visa Annual Report in 2019 (https://usa.visa.com/content/dam/VCOM/regional/na/us/run-your-business/documents/visa-state-of-entrepreneurship-research-summary.pdf). In the United States, 16% of start-ups have at least one female founder. Interestingly, 90.3% of women run micro-businesses, which play a substantial role in the economy, generating an average of $1.8 trillion annually. However, 61% of women find funding challenging, and two-thirds rely on self-funding due to the gender funding gap, where less than 2% of venture capital goes to women. These numbers emphasize the need to address these disparities and empower women entrepreneurs.

In this chapter, you'll encounter women from various industries, proving that being a tech founder is just one facet of entrepreneurship. Technology can enhance any business today, and these women are leading the way in their own unique paths. Although there are fewer traditionally defined "tech founders" among them, it's not due to a lack of entrepreneurial spirit but rather a scarcity of tech skills. Bridging this skills gap and increasing access to funding could be transformative, but for now, these women are already shaping a brighter future.

Overcoming Roadblocks

As female founders we face many of the same roadblocks and hit up against them over and over. The women you will see featured in this chapter have encountered and surmounted several common hurdles on their entrepreneurial journeys. They have found ways to work around them and keep going by harnessing grit, persistence, and working with others. These roadblocks are shared here so you can know that you are not alone when you are building and run into them as well, because likely you will. The following are the top roadblocks these women faced:

- **Hiring the right people:** Assembling a dedicated team that shares your vision is a foundational challenge. It can be hard to have the time and knowledge to find the best people when you are on limited funds and time. These women have pushed through and found creative ways to find good team members.
- **Not taken seriously enough:** Facing gender and age biases in technical fields, these entrepreneurs have confidently taken on leadership roles, challenging stereotypes.
- **Managing under constraints:** Many have managed teams with limited resources, showcasing their resourcefulness and commitment to their ventures.
- **Funding and fundraising:** The gender funding gap hasn't deterred them. They persist in their fundraising efforts, undaunted by rejection.
- **Marketing and sales:** They've developed effective marketing and sales strategies, conveying their value propositions convincingly.
- **Sustainable growth:** Balancing growth with sustainability is a complex task they've navigated thoughtfully.
- **Avoiding burnout:** Recognizing the importance of self-care, they've established strategies to maintain their well-being while driving their businesses forward.
- **Confronting gender bias:** These founders have confronted bias head-on, challenging stereotypes and paving the way for future generations of women.

- **Loneliness:** Entrepreneurship can be isolating, but these women have sought support networks to combat loneliness.
- **Building self-confidence:** Overcoming self-doubt has been a transformative journey. Their experiences highlight the power of self-belief.

These women's stories are a testament to their resilience and determination. They've used these roadblocks as stepping stones, redefining what's possible. They're not just rewriting their destinies, they're creating a more inclusive and equitable future for all aspiring entrepreneurs, regardless of gender or background. Their journey showcases the power of persistence, courage, and the unwavering pursuit of dreams.

Women Building

In this section, we celebrate the resilience and vision of female founders who are charting new territories in the realms of building for the future. These mini interviews provide a window into the lives of women who have turned obstacles into opportunities. From overcoming stereotypes to building innovative products, their stories are not just narratives of success but blueprints for the future.

Tech/SaaS

In the fast-paced world of tech and SaaS, remarkable women are paving the way for innovation. Meet the trailblazers who are pushing boundaries and redefining possibilities in this dynamic industry. Many of them, not necessarily technical experts from the start, embraced the "just dangerous enough" mentality, delving into the tech world and figuring out a way to build. These extraordinary women share a common vision: a future where technology knows no bounds and where women stand at the forefront of innovation. Join us as we delve into their journeys, challenges, and dreams, all of which are shaping the future of the tech and SaaS landscape.

Founder: Meryem Arik

Company: TitanML

Product: *We are building a platform that makes LLM models significantly cheaper and faster to deploy—even on small GPUs. This will accelerate the adoption of AI while reducing the environmental impact of that AI.*

Industry: AI/LLMs

Stage: Seed

Funding: VC backed

What needs to happen for more women to build the future? Part of the solution is that women need to be encouraged to do technical degrees. If we don't have a good pipeline of excellent technical and smart women coming up, then we are always going to see fewer women founders in tech.

■　■　■

Founder: Angie Moody

Company: Ruby Money

Product: *Ruby Money is on a mission to put more time and money in the hands of female entrepreneurs. My product simplifies taxes and helps you save for retirement. It's designed specifically for freelancers, consultants, and soloprenuers.*

Industry: FinTech

Stage: Pre-seed, started 2021

Funding: Venture capital

What needs to happen for more women to build the future?
A massive change in the expectations for what "makes a good entrepreneur," a ton more funding flowing into the hands of women investors, and women themselves giving less fucks being okay with the risk of failure in public.

■ ■ ■

Founder: Bridget Harris

Company: You Can Book Me

Product: *Our software is about providing free/low-cost appointment software, which helps small businesses, education, and businesses book appointments with their customers.*

Industry: Small business software

Stage: SaaS/B2B2C

Funding: Bootstrapped, since 2011

What needs to happen for more women to build the future?
Less sexism! The barriers women face are structural, economic, institutional, and cultural, and maintained by a deeply patriarchal society around the world. The only way women will share equal parts in building the future is by increasing education at an early age for all children on gender stereotypes and unconscious bias, which reinforces these barriers.

■ ■ ■

Founder: Nisreen Hasib

Company: Signoff

Product: *Signoff's mission is to create a world in which all people have safe, secure, and beautiful housing. Our inaugural product* *matches designers and architects with general contractors, with a focus on matching people that have compatible working styles, so they are able to develop successful, long-term partnerships. To build the present and future in which all people have safe, secure, and beautiful housing, we must support our designers, builders, and tradespeople by giving them the tools they need to build and scale their businesses.*

Industry: PropTech/real estate

Stage: Pre-seed

Funding: Venture capital

What needs to happen for more women to build the future?
We must take women seriously. That is easy to say, but not a lot of people do it. I was talking with another female founder, and both of us wondered, "What would have happened if Facebook was pitched by a woman, instead of a man?" It was easy to picture the idea being dismissed out of hand as a silly way for girls to connect with friends, rather than the genesis for a platform that would dominate the social media world.

■ ■ ■

Founder: Rosario B. Casas

Company: BCPartners Tech, XR Americas, and Brooklyn2 Bogota Digital Transformation Community

Product: *We work for a future in which the correct use of digital tools and technology allows founders to build better and grow bigger, increasing their positive impact. We believe in the use of technology to improve economic growth. And for that we have three businesses: BCPartners Tech, XR Americas, and Brooklyn 2Bogota Digital Transformation Community.*

Industry: AR/VR/AI

Stage: Bootstrapping

Funding: Bootstrapping

What needs to happen for more women to build the future?
More education, better and more tangible role models for teenagers, access to resources, and a phenomenal supporting network—mentors, sponsors, and so on.

Health

In the realm of health, women entrepreneurs are leading the charge, developing groundbreaking solutions to improve well-being and redefine the future of health care. These visionaries have a common thread woven through their stories—a relentless pursuit of change.

These remarkable women share a similar vision—an inclusive future in which technology, empathy, and innovation intersect to empower everyone. Their journeys encompass diverse domains, yet they all face similar challenges, such as navigating gender biases and seeking equitable funding. Dive into their narratives and discover the transformative power of women in the health industry.

Founder: Kendra Koch

Company: Touchy Feely

Product: *I am building a marketplace to help highly sensitive or neurodivergent people find everything they need to foster sensory wellness while also building a judgment-free zone where people can share their experiences and swap strategies to help combat loneliness and erase mental health stigma.*

Industry: Mental health and wellness for the neurodivergent population

Stage: Bootstrapping, founded 2023

Funding: Bootstrapping

What needs to happen for more women to build the future?
In order to help build the future, women need space and support to create in a feminine way versus just trying to play on the same level as men. We are connectors, not competitors, and need room to build collaboratively. Also, access to affordable, quality childcare is essential, too.

■ ■ ■

Founder: Lindsey Williams

Company: My UTI

Product: *We are building a better future for women who suffer from frequent urinary tract infections. Frequent and chronic UTIs are often dismissed as a "women's issue" with women being shamed for sexual activity and hygiene as triggers rather than looking deeper into causality. Research in this area is lacking and women are frustrated with the dismissive care they receive. MyUTI offers direct access to advanced (PCR) testing for the top 12 symptom causing pathogens with an antibiotic recommendation based on pathogens and resistance genes detected in the sample. The goal is to empower women to control their care, leverage data and insights to positively affect research in this area of women's health (especially as it relates to menopause), and ultimately affect outcomes.*

Industry: Women's health

Stage: Pre-seed

Funding: Angel investors

What needs to happen for more women to build the future?
It's so simple, but just *believe women.* I was recently at an

investor showcase where a man was pitching his company and was being questioned on the market demand for their planned product line expansion. His response was "I guess you'll just have to trust me." It was like a knife to my chest because I knew I could never stand up and say that. The majority of men in the room couldn't directly understand the pain point I'm solving for, simply because they don't have vulvas. So I have to spend extra time justifying the need (almost like justifying our own existence) above and beyond market and scientific data, meanwhile a man says "just trust me." Oh—and that company got the investment.

■ ■ ■

Founder: Jodi Klaristenfeld

Company: FLRRiSH, Inc.

Product: *I am helping empower, educate, and support preemie and NICU families on their journey through the NICU and beyond. NICU families are often lumped together with full-term parents and our journey is completely different. I believe if we get parents the necessary tools to navigate this most challenging yet rewarding journey from the outset, the better off they will be in all aspects of their life. Over 80% of all parents with children in the NICU experience some type of mental health issue within the first seven years of their child's life. Preparing them how to change their mindset can only help decrease that number instead of growing it.*

Industry: NICU and preemie parent wellness

Stage: Bootstrapping

Funding: Bootstrapping

What needs to happen for more women to build the future?
I think more key decision-makers need to ask working

women and moms what it is they really need most and actually listen to them. Instead of always looking at the bottom-line cost of programs, it is important to look at the actual impact of the programs. Impact is what makes something successful, not just money.

■ ■ ■

Founder: Julie Laux

Company: 101 Before One

Product: *We help parents introduce solids to their baby with our signature family meals from the start program. Parents are guided on how to cook and serve healthy, nutritious whole food meals to their baby versus serving them processed jars of baby food. This is the next generation that will appreciate whole foods and have diverse palates.*

Industry: Baby nutrition

Stage: Bootstrapping

Funding: Bootstrapping

What needs to happen for more women to build the future? A supportive community that helps women (and moms) connect with other women. For example, you may be good at one thing but need help in a certain area to outsource for your business.

■ ■ ■

Founder: Sehreen Noor Ali

Company: Sleuth

Product: We're transforming children's health through better information, leveraging the crowdsourced wisdom and AI.

Sleuth enables parents to understand, track, and predict their child's health.

Industry: Children's health and AI

Stage: Pre-seed

Funding: Venture capital

What needs to happen for more women to build the future? I think women need to play their own game and not feel pigeonholed into the off-the-shelf narratives peddled in the media about what start-ups and founders should look like.

■ ■ ■

Founder: Dr. Melissa Barker

Company: The Phoenix Project

Product: *Phoenix is an intelligent AI advocate for your mental health bringing the best healing practices and tools to your fingertips.*

Industry: Mental health/psychedelics/ AI

Stage: Pre-seed

Funding: Angel investors

What needs to happen for more women to build the future? More access to capital, network support, and community.

Education

Education, a realm ripe for disruption and innovation, is witnessing profound change instigated by visionary women entrepreneurs. Within this dynamic sector, numerous challenges beg for solutions. Access to quality education, the empowerment of marginalized communities, and the democratization of knowledge are just a few of the pressing issues these pioneers aim to address.

The following trailblazers are demolishing barriers and propelling change within their respective domains. Although their missions vary across different facets of education, they are united by common challenges. They seek increased mentorship opportunities, greater diversity among investors, and the creation of more visible female role models. Their stories are a testament to the transformative impact women are driving in the field of education.

Founder: Ali Buckland

Company: Skizaa Education

Product: *At Skizaa Education, we are bridging the gap between teachers in rural, slum, and last-mile classrooms across sub-Saharan Africa and the organizations that fund them. We support NGOs, foundations, and other stakeholders to collect and analyze education data quickly and cost effectively, whilst also empowering the teachers collecting this data.*

Industry: Education

Stage: Pre-seed

Funding: Angel investors

What needs to happen for more women to build the future? We need more mentorship for female entrepreneurs, especially for those working in emerging markets. There also needs to be more women responsible for allocating capital—my female angel investors have been so instrumental in my growth at Skizaa.

■ ■ ■

Founder: Ashima Sharma

Company: Dreami

Product: *Dreami powers data-driven career development programs for the 36 million people in the US who face barriers to employment.*

Industry: EdTech

Stage: Seed

Funding: Angel investors

What needs to happen for more women to build the future? More diverse investors—the people writing the checks need to diversify ASAP in order to have more women funded to build the future, and not worry about health insurance/childcare/and so on.

■ ■ ■

Founder: Meredith Noble

Company: Learn Grant Writing

Product: *We built the Global Grant Writers Collective to help women needing a more flexible career to become well-paid grant writing consultants.*

Industry: Education

Stage: Bootstrapped

Funding: Bootstrapped

What needs to happen for more women to build the future? We need to see it to believe it. The more examples we can provide, the more those serve as a beacon of lighthouse inspiration.

Consumer Packaged Goods (CPG)

These trailblazing CPG innovators are transforming the industry, guided by a steadfast commitment to sustainability and inclusivity. As they pioneer this change, their journeys bring common challenges and pressing issues to the forefront.

In their pursuit of a more sustainable and inclusive future in the CPG realm, these entrepreneurs confront shared hurdles. They advocate for empathy in the workplace and support for caregivers, echoing the broader demand for a balanced work-life paradigm. Furthermore, their stories highlight the significance of recognizing and harnessing the skills honed through caregiving, emphasizing their remarkable versatility.

To empower more women to shape the future of CPG, these visionary leaders stress the importance of acknowledging competent female talent, guaranteeing equitable access to financial resources and educational opportunities, and dismantling systemic biases entrenched across industries. Their journeys serve as a potent reminder that advocating for and bolstering female-founded brands is not mere rhetoric but a tangible stride toward cultivating a fairer business landscape.

Founder: Ada Chen

Company: Chuan's Promise

Product: *Chuan's Promise (new name TBA) is a natural skincare brand focused on sustainability and inclusivity. We're changing the beauty industry from the inside out with our approach to sustainability through product packaging and formulation: our products are packaged in compostable and recyclable materials, and formulated using high-quality, ethically sourced organic ingredients. Our goal is to make the eco-friendly choice an easy decision when customers shop for new skincare and body products.*

Industry: CPG/DTC e-commerce—Natural skincare and beauty

Stage: Bootstrapping

Funding: Bootstrapping

What needs to happen for more women to build the future? I believe we need more empathy in the workplace in order for more women to be able to build the future—whether they achieve it by rising through the ranks or starting their own businesses. We need to train managers and leadership teams on how to support caregivers, and we need to provide more resources for those who are juggling their work and caregiving responsibilities. As a society, we need to recognize that the skills gained from caregiving—like attention to detail and clear communication—are valuable outside of a caregiving setting.

■ ■ ■

Founder: Stephanie Franklin

Company: Fly Wines

Product: *We are committed to building a wine company that champions diversity and inclusion, with the aim of creating equitable opportunities within the wine industry. To achieve this, we prioritize working with independent wineries from around the world, especially those owned or operated by individuals from underrepresented communities. This not only enriches the variety of wines we offer but also supports economic growth in diverse settings. By doing so, we believe we are contributing to a more inclusive and sustainable future.*

Industry: Wine

Stage: Bootstrapping

Funding: Bootstrapping

What needs to happen for more women to build the future? For more women to build the future, it's crucial that they are recognized as competent leaders without needing validation from men. But this alone isn't enough. Women also need equal access to financial resources and educational opportunities, especially in fields that are shaping the future like technology and science. Policies that encourage work-life balance can make a significant difference, as can mentorship programs that connect aspiring female entrepreneurs with established leaders. Moreover, combating systemic biases, such as the gender pay gap and discriminatory practices, will help create a more level playing field. By focusing on these areas, we can empower young women to become business owners and leaders who don't have to second-guess their decisions or their worth.

■ ■ ■

Founder: Carrie Sporer

Company: SWAIR

Product: *SWAIR's hero product is Showerless Shampoo. My cofounder and I created this product because there was nothing on the market that could clean very sweaty hair short of a traditional in-shower shampoo and blow dry. We felt frustrated that we needed to cut workouts short or even skip them in order to accommodate our hair. Now we offer women a solution to go from sweaty to ready in five minutes or less, and we also have additional audiences with children who have trouble with getting their hair wet and people who are unable to shower regularly for medical reasons. There really is no shortage of people who can use this shortcut to make their "getting ready" process easier and more efficient.*

Industry: Haircare (beauty/CPG)

Stage: Bootstrapping

Funding: Bootstrapping

What needs to happen for more women to build the future?
Where to begin? There are *so* many things on macro and micro levels, but I am happy to share what has been most beneficial for SWAIR. I have met hundreds of men that offered to "help" in different capacities since starting my entrepreneurial journey, but I can think of only five in particular that have actually stepped up. Each of them has been incredibly generous with their time, connections, and feedback for no benefit of their own. They are believers in the brand and want to see us succeed. I think more people of influence need to champion female-founded brands by providing real support and not just paying lip service to the cause.

Media

In the realm of media, these visionary founders are driving a significant shift toward diverse representation, inclusivity, and social change. Their journeys are characterized by a collective commitment to reshaping the media landscape, making it more reflective of our diverse society.

As they endeavor to create a media world where diversity is the norm, not a tokenized gesture, these entrepreneurs are united by common themes and vital issues. They emphasize the importance of providing role models and mentors to aspiring women in the field, fostering communities that offer support, insights, and opportunities, and demanding equal opportunities and expectations for women, especially women of color.

These media innovators are amplifying underrepresented voices, from those wrongfully convicted to mothers and those silenced in the justice system to marginalized communities in entertainment and South Asian narratives in filmmaking. Their stories underscore the transformative power of diversity and inclusion, and the necessity of women, particularly women of color, occupying positions of influence and decision-making in the media industry.

Founder: Jill Koziol

Company: Motherly, Inc.

Product: *Motherly believes that when a mother thrives, families and communities thrive. As such our mission to empower mothers to thrive providing holistic content, community, and commerce solutions will better our future. We currently engage 40M mothers each month on the journey of motherhood from conception to college.*

Industry: Media and e-commerce

Stage: Series B

Funding: Venture capital

What needs to happen for more women to build the future? We need more women in investing positions and affordable childcare solutions to enable mothers the time and space to innovate.

■ ■ ■

Founder: Rachel Nussbaum

Company: Specular TV

Product: *I am building a business where diverse representation in video (both corporate marketing and entertainment) is a norm, not a tokenized effort. Living in a truly diverse and inclusive community means we all feel like we belong. As an executive producer, one way to achieve belonging is to create content representing* *all races and genders so kids growing up watch superheroes, chefs, artists, and business leaders who look and sound like them.*

Industry: Marketing and entertainment

Stage: Bootstrapping

Funding: Bootstrapping

What needs to happen for more women to build the future?
They need to hear more success stories of other women who did that. They need more mentors and communities where they can receive support, gain insights, access potential clients, and support one another.

■ ■ ■

Founder: Jia Wertz

Company: Amina Fire Productions

Product: *When I decided to make documentary films, I knew I wanted to focus on wrongful convictions—a global issue that the majority of the general public doesn't seem to realize the gravity of. Approximately 2% to 10% of all the people incarcerated in our country are actually innocent. This means that of the 2.3 million people in our prisons, up to 230,000 are innocent. Bringing attention to this cause not only helps amplify the voices of innocent people who have been unjustly silenced but also raises awareness so we are hopefully better equipped to prevent wrongful incarceration in the future.*

Industry: Filmmaking

Stage: Bootstrapped

Funding: Bootstrapped

What needs to happen for more women to build the future?
We need to give women the same opportunities as men

have, and hold women to the same expectations. Often women are much more highly scrutinized and yet, also given much more responsibility. In the film industry, women are extremely underrepresented—of the top 250 grossing films of 2022, only 11% had female directors. And the same goes for other roles as well, comprising only 7% of cinematographers, 19% of writers, 25% of executive producers, and 31% of producers in 2022.

My voice not only represents a much-needed female narrative in the film industry but also that of the South Asian population, which is underrepresented. Blending the experiences and talents of different individuals, especially women, can be very powerful, as we've recently witnessed with the Barbie movie, which became Warner Bros.' highest grossing global release in history. It's great that diversity is getting far more attention than ever before, but there is still a long way to go, and by bringing in more minority and female voices into filmmaking, we are moving in the right direction.

■ ■ ■

Founder: Kacie Lett Gordon

Company: IT ALL Media

Product: *We're a womxn-centered media company using story and conversation to create social change. What started as a podcast, turned into grounded theory research, curriculum, original content/media (podcast, short films, conferences, event activations, and tv shows).*

Industry: Media

Stage: Bootstrapping

Funding: Bootstrapped

What needs to happen for more women to build the future?
Women, and especially women of color, to be in positions of power.

Human Resources/Consulting/Coworking

In the dynamic domains of human resources, consulting, and coworking, these innovative founders are spearheading change. They share a vision of a future that's more empowering and collaborative for women. Their journeys are marked by the creation of spaces, resources, and opportunities that amplify women's voices and champion underrepresented perspectives.

To enable more women to shape this future, they advocate for transparency and open networking. They emphasize the importance of mentorship programs and strong professional networks to bridge gender gaps in leadership roles. These founders are building communities where aspirations are celebrated, not just achievable.

Whether it's advancing careers, establishing coworking hubs, or mentoring the next generation of leaders, these founders are rewriting the script of success. Their stories showcase the transformative power of collaboration, mentorship, and a shared commitment to a future where women hold significant influence across various domains of work and beyond.

Founder: Ashley Louise

Company: Ladies Get Paid

Product: *We teach women how to advance in their careers and grow their wealth.*

Industry: Career and personal finance

Stage: Bootstrapping

Funding: Bootstrapped

What needs to happen for more women to build the future?
More women with more money, more power, and more
knowledge.

■ ■ ■

Founder: Catherine Hover

Company: Palette

Product: *Palette is a resource for women to unapologetically
advance themselves in business and in life. A place where
women and allies can come together to support each other without judgment or fear that their dreams are not achievable.*

Industry: Coworking and community

Stage: Bootstrapping

Funding: Bootstrapped

What needs to happen for more women to build the future?
To get more women engaged in building the future, we
need more transparency and open networking with the
women already in the arena. There are so many women at
various levels and backgrounds who want to be involved
and simply need to be invited in. I am thrilled to be part of
that invitation and open the door for others to contribute
and support a new way of building the future of work.

■ ■ ■

Founder: Moriya Kassis

Company: Product League

Product: *A mentoring program for [tech] product managers. Our
mentoring program is designed to empower product managers to*

rediscover their passion for their work and find a sense of purpose that transcends the traditional career ladder. Ultimately, our vision is to create a community that prioritizes people and focuses on building products that truly matter. By helping professionals find meaning in their careers and develop essential skills, we believe we are contributing to a future where work is more than just a means to an end—it's a pathway to personal and collective fulfillment and progress.

Industry: Mentoring

Stage: Bootstrapping

Funding: Bootstrapped

What needs to happen for more women to build the future?
To enable more women to actively participate in building the future, several key factors should be considered and addressed, especially mentorship and networking. Building mentorship programs and fostering strong professional networks can provide women with guidance, support, and opportunities for growth. This can help bridge the gender gap in leadership roles.

Learning from Others

Reading the profiles of these remarkable women who are actively shaping the future is inspiring and enlightening. Their journeys, filled with challenges and triumphs, remind us that we are not alone in our entrepreneurial endeavors. These women are living proof that with determination and resilience, we can overcome the roadblocks that stand in our way.

Their experiences provide valuable lessons and insights, offering a wealth of knowledge that we can all draw from as we navigate our own paths. As we read about their journeys, we gain the wisdom to confront adversity, build strong teams, and foster the self-confidence needed to thrive in any industry.

Perhaps most important, their stories underscore the significance of collaboration. As women entrepreneurs, we can achieve so much more by working together, supporting one another, and breaking down the barriers that have held us back for far too long. It's a future where ego takes a back seat to unity, where shared goals and shared successes become the norm.

But this is just the beginning. In Chapter 12, we will delve even deeper into the concept of collaboration and explore how, by joining forces, we can build a brighter, more inclusive future for all. Together, we can turn our individual entrepreneurial equations into a collective force for change, advancing not only our own businesses but also the cause of gender equality in entrepreneurship. As we read about the profiles of women who have paved the way, we'll discover that collaboration isn't just a choice; it's a powerful tool for transformation.

Code Review: Women Building

For this chapter, I collected and reviewed the insights and experiences of remarkable women who are actively building the future. Similar to debugging a complex code base, I carefully examined their journeys, identified roadblocks, reviewed their visions for the future, and assessed their recommendations for creating a more inclusive environment for women in entrepreneurship. For this review I want to turn some of that back on you to reflect on as well, because you are also a woman building the future; let's dive in:

- **Founders' roadblocks:** Just as a developer would identify bugs in code, we asked these founders about their roadblocks. What challenges have you faced on your entrepreneurial journey? Are there recurring obstacles that you have encountered? Did you have similar struggles as they did?

- **Building for the future:** Similar to reviewing code for its functionality, we've explored what these women are building for the future. What are your goals and visions? How do you see your work shaping the world?
- **Creating a supportive environment:** Similar to fixing code issues, we inquired about their suggestions for improving the environment for women entrepreneurs. What do you believe needs to be done to make it better and more accessible for other women to follow their path and build for the future?
- **Learning from each other:** Just as developers learn from code reviews, I asked these founders if they learned from reviewing the profiles and experiences of their peers. Did you find relatable stories that made you feel less alone in their journey?

By conducting this review, I hope that you see you are not alone in this journey of building, that others face similar struggles but together we can build a brighter tomorrow. In Chapter 12 we will dive further into how you can build more effectively alongside other women.

12

Building the Future Together

The Code of Collaboration

The best advice that I could give other women entrepreneurs, especially women in tech, is to find a tribe.

—Natasia Malihollo

ENTERING THE WORLD of tech and start-ups can often feel like diving into the intricate world of coding. At first glance, it might seem like a solitary endeavor, with lines of code resembling the building blocks of a digital realm. However, as any coder knows, the most robust and efficient software doesn't emerge from a single developer toiling in isolation. It's the result of collaboration, feedback loops, and a collective effort to create something greater than the sum of its parts.

When I ventured into this dynamic arena, I was pleasantly surprised by the collaborative nature of the journey. Contrary to the notion that the tech world can be cutthroat, I discovered a community where women actively supported each other's endeavors. It echoed the spirit of collaborative coding, where developers from diverse backgrounds join forces to solve complex problems. Although the world may portray us as competitors, I found that women in tech were more inclined toward collaboration. Just as programmers share code to build remarkable software, women entrepreneurs unite to construct a brighter future.

In this chapter, we'll explore the art of building together, much like developers crafting lines of code that weave into functional applications. We'll delve into the power of collaboration, the importance of setting aside our egos, and the transformative impact of pooling our resources and knowledge. Just as every coder relies on a community of developers and libraries to build remarkable software, every woman entrepreneur thrives within a supportive network. So, let's embark on this journey together, uncovering the strategies that will help us not only build together but also shape a future where women lead, innovate, and inspire—a future much like a well-coded application: robust, efficient, and driven by a collective vision.

The camaraderie and resilience of my fellow founders, who have stood by my side over the years, have been my pillars of strength. Their pep talks, unwavering support, and a shared commitment to collaboration over competition have sustained me through the most challenging moments of my entrepreneurial journey. Although we pursued distinct business ventures across various industries, we were, in many ways, building alongside one another.

Our businesses were at similar stages, and we encountered analogous challenges. We understood the profound solitude that can accompany entrepreneurship and recognized the importance of coming together. As communal beings, and as women, we possess a unique capacity for empathy and nurturing. To truly thrive, we knew we had to build together.

I've been a part of countless female founder groups and online and in-person communities. However, none fully encapsulated the vision I held for a supportive network of fellow builders. I was searching for what type of community or support I needed to thrive as a business owner, so I started asking successful business owners what they were doing. I did this through interviewing several amazing female business owners on my podcast throughout the years and one of those interviews was with Dana Spinola, founder and CEO of Fab'rik. Her interview led me to make a change in the support I sought:

Dana Spinola
Founder and CEO of Fab'rik

Allobee Radio, Episode 52

Dana has led her company with such a focus on mission and values and that is something that I admire greatly. It is not easy to do and especially as the company grows as hers has done over the years. Not only has she stayed consistent, but she also built this thriving company all while raising a family of her own.

Brooke: Dana, in moments when you feel down or overwhelmed, how do you center yourself or rebuild your confidence?

Dana: To combat those feelings, I turn to what I've termed *my wise counsel*. It's essential to clarify that these aren't just my regular friends, though I cherish each of them. Some friends will always champion and encourage you, and while that's lovely, I especially value those who challenge me to improve. That's what I usually seek.

   My wise counsel consists of individuals who might not even know each other personally. I group them on a text thread, and whenever I need genuine, unfiltered advice, they're my go-to. They're the kind who'll let me know if there's spinach stuck between my teeth or if I'm deviating from my authentic self. When I approach them with a new idea or challenge, they provide insights that align with my core values and intentions, even if it's not what I initially want to hear.

There's immense comfort in having people in your life who offer that kind of clarity, revealing blind spots you might have missed.

Furthermore, my faith anchors me. I regularly seek wisdom from esteemed leaders, and more often than not, I delve into the Bible. It's like going straight to the source for guidance. But as valuable as divine wisdom is, having earthly confidants who candidly remind me when I'm straying off course is something I truly cherish.

Drawing inspiration from Dana Spinola's wise council concept, I forged my version: a founder council. It was a group of women who were also founders, representing various stages of business. These were the people I could vent my frustrations to, who challenged me when necessary, and who reminded me that I wasn't alone in this journey. They became the bedrock of my entrepreneurial life.

My founder council was pivotal, not only in facilitating the acquisition of my company but also in providing unwavering support during the most trying periods of my life. They stood by me when my husband faced unemployment, when my health deteriorated due to burnout, when book deals were on the horizon, and even as potential customers came my way. They were there for late-night texts, midday phone calls, and a profound sense of camaraderie. I believe that every founder should have a similar council, and it's now my mission to help other women build theirs. In the start-up arena, where all players are fighting for survival, we are equals, regardless of experience. Start-ups, by their nature, present similar challenges.

I share this concept of a founder council because I believe that having this support system in place while you build can be a game-changer. I want to share some tangible ways in which having a founder council and building together with fellow founders significantly affected my life.

Prioritizing Health and Well-Being

One significant area of transformation in my life was my approach to health and well-being. The challenges of building during a pandemic took a toll on my health, as it did for many others. However, witnessing how members of my founder council prioritized their health amid their entrepreneurial pursuits served as a powerful motivator.

Two of my founder's council members really stood out when it came to health prioritization: Amanda Goetz, founder of House of Wise, and Blessing Adesiyan, founder of MH WorkLife. They both demonstrated daily how to take control of one's health. They had learned through their building experience that it was very easy to fall into burnout and let your health go, so they shifted their mindset and made it a priority. Their journeys, which included CrossFit, yoga, running, lifting, and mindfulness practices, inspired me to focus on my own health. I wish I had made this shift sooner but it was not until after a year of burnout in 2022 and the acquisition that I would start to focus on my health and well-being. I put it off because I felt everything in my life was more important than my own health, and I could not have been more wrong. This is something that should be talked about more in the world of founders. I hope that by sharing a small look into my own journey that it will help others.

After the acquisition, I embarked on a year-long journey of self-improvement, resulting in a 100-pound weight loss, relief from chronic inflammation, and improved mental health. I started treating my body with respect and more like an athlete would. I wanted to be able to show up for my family for a long time to come, and also have the endurance to build again one day. Building a company is like running a marathon for years. I needed to be in shape mentally and physically to do that. I started doing yoga and Pilates, but also took up running. I did not just focus on physical activity but also nourished my body better, took time to get more sleep and spend more time unplugged from my phone. I also really focused in on the GEMS framework and nourished each element to become stronger.

Through this journey of health prioritization, I realized that I really missed building and working on a passion and product that I loved, and I searched for hobbies and other ways to find passions outside of work, yet I truly missed building. My friend Blessing told me that "the work we do, we should not have to take a vacation from," and that hit me hard one day this last summer. I knew that what was on the horizon for me needed to be aligned with my passion. Right now, my passion lies in helping women build and also building myself. I needed to get back to that, and that is why a year after the acquisition I decided to take the leap back into entrepreneurship. There are many unknowns and I am not sure exactly what I am building yet, but I am feeling the flame of passion reignite and that I am healthier and more prepared to build again.

If our passion is fueling us the right way and we still love what we are building, it should not burn us to the ground; it should feel like a vacation. Observing fellow founders who balanced health and business success nudged me to make this profound shift, and I am forever grateful. Having that inspiration from your founder council can be a game-changer as a founder.

Trusting Intuition and Protecting Energy

Another vital lesson was learning to trust my intuition and protect my energy. Balancing the demands of customers, team members, investors, and others can be overwhelming. As entrepreneurs, we tend to prioritize everything else over ourselves. This led to exhaustion and decision-making that sometimes ran contrary to our instincts. I wish I had spent more time focusing on this while I was building Allobee, but I did not realize how valuable it was until I was in the midst of the acquisition process. I was super drained at this point in 2022 after not being able to fundraise and trying to keep the company going, but I knew I had to keep going to make the acquisition happen. After the acquisition I was brought on as the chief product officer at The Riveter and my identity shifted from being a founder to being an employee, and that was something that I was not fully prepared for. For so many years my identity was, Brooke, founder and CEO of Allobee, and now I was Brooke, chief product officer at The Riveter. In some ways a lot of pressure was taken away from me moving into an employee role, but also now I was not building a company, I was integrating into a company. This was something I had not done in a long time, having been an entrepreneur for so many years up to that point. I was a bit lost, so I turned to my founder council for support on this.

Two members of my founder council played crucial roles in this transformation. During my journey of wellness and focusing more on my health, I came across a concept called Human Design, thanks to my friend Andrea. Andrea Berg is a corporate professional turned Human Design Coach, and she helped me understand my energy better and trust my instincts. Human Design is a system that combines elements of astrology, the I Ching, Kabbalah, and the chakra system, among others, to create a unique personality profile for individuals. It's often used for self-discovery, personal growth, and making decisions in alignment with one's true nature.

She helped me realize I am a projector, in Human Design terminology, and showed me how my energy works but also how I best interact with others. A projector in Human Design is one of the four main types of individuals (the others being manifestor, generator, and reflector). Projectors are known for their ability to guide and manage the energy of others rather than initiating action themselves. They often excel in roles where they can offer advice, insight, and direction. Projectors tend to work best when they are recognized and invited to participate in activities rather than pushing themselves into projects or situations. Recognizing their unique role and working in alignment with it can lead to greater success and fulfillment for projectors. My conversations with Andrea on this led me to a lot of realizations and to making shifts in my life that have helped me be more productive and healthier.

Another helpful founder council member has been Danya Shults, my executive coach, whom I brought on during the acquisition process and who has helped me to prioritize my needs and navigate my shifting identity from founder and CEO to employee. I knew I had put so much aside while I built, and she helped me to rediscover where I wanted to focus my energy and exploration. These women enabled me to slow down and listen to my intuition, rather than relentlessly pushing forward. They also showed me that I have a lot of living and building still to do.

Surrounding myself with a council of fellow founders who aligned with my values not only made me a better leader but also gave me insights into my future as I transitioned from CEO and founder of Allobee to an employee, and eventually back into entrepreneurship. The shift back into entrepreneurship is new and something I will still be navigating for a while. I do not want to operate the same way I did before, but move forward with the knowledge of the learned experiences and lessons that are now ingrained in me and build in a better way. We do not know what we do not know when we start out as entrepreneurs, and even though I have spent a lot of time as one over the last 10 years, I am still learning. This time around I do feel much more equipped with following my GEMS framework, having a founder council, focusing on my health, and having one acquisition under my belt. I am slowly building what my next entrepreneurial equation looks like and know that the passion will continue to fuel my way. I do plan to build more in public this time and share more about the earliest days of building. I believe we do not share this enough as founders because we do not want others to see any weak points. Throughout this new phase of discerning whether to take the leap back into entrepreneurship, I have leaned heavily on my founder council, and I am grateful to have had them. They helped me realize that my passion lies in building and helping others build. I knew this deep down, but it helps to hear it from others. I encourage you to consider who in your life could be part of your founder council, such as business owners you admire and have crossed paths with. If none come to mind, I urge you to join our community at Built x Women (details in the resource section). This book isn't just meant to inspire you; it's designed to help you build the future. To do that, you need support, and it's much more effective when you build alongside others.

Egos Aside: Collaborating over Competing

Despite the prevailing spirit of collaboration in the world of entrepreneurship, egos can sometimes obstruct our path. The scarcity mindset in funding, particularly for women, can lead us to guard our opportunities and connections. We might even view other women entrepreneurs as competitors, vying for the same sliver of the pie or the same potential sponsors. There were a few times founders told me no, purely because of the fact we were in slight competition. They were not the only ones who said no; I definitely turned opportunities down for the same reason and looking back, I wish I had collaborated more with other women-owned brands.

Collaboration over competition is not just a catchy phrase; it's a philosophy that, if embraced, can yield incredible results. We must set aside our egos, even as ambitious women eager for our businesses to succeed. Building a product requires more than just technical skills; it necessitates an entire team. To build the future, all of us are indispensable, and there's no room for egos to impede our progress.

Build Together: The New Era of Building

We find ourselves in a new era of building, armed with tools like AI and no-code solutions that empower us to work more efficiently. Many women are no longer content with the 9-to-5 corporate ladder climb; they are leaving traditional jobs at an astounding rate, eager to create something meaningful. Although building is an enticing option, building in isolation is not the answer.

Building together is the path to success. We must share resources, connections, and knowledge generously, raising one another up. My conversations with women building businesses have revealed that many of their challenges boil down to two key roadblocks: a lack of support and a lack of knowledge. These barriers can be overcome through collaboration, setting aside our egos, and working together to shape the future. When building gets tough, we need each other to prevail.

How Do We Build Together? Seven Strategies

Through my experiences in building a founder council and working with hundreds of female founders, I've identified seven strategies that I believe can enable women not just to build together but to genuinely craft a brighter future for us all:

- **Buildathons:** Unlike traditional hackathons that may be inaccessible for many, especially mothers, buildathons offer a more inclusive approach. If you are not familiar with a hackathon it is a fast, tech-focused competition where people work together to solve problems in a short time, like a day or weekend, in person. Buildathons however, can be held virtually, during accessible hours, or in-person at coworking spaces over shorter periods. The focus here is on iterating ideas with the goal of developing projects that extend beyond the event.

- **Getting creative with funding:** The traditional venture capital model doesn't fit everyone. There are various innovative approaches to funding, some of which are yet to be explored fully. Funding doesn't necessarily have to be financial; knowledge-sharing, grant applications, partnerships, and sponsorships can be alternative routes.

- **Mentor moments:** Mentorship doesn't always have to be a long-term commitment. It can manifest as mentor moments: brief yet impactful interactions where experienced founders offer guidance and support when needed. These moments can be powerful, both for mentors and mentees.

- **Perfect the ask:** Women sometimes hesitate to make clear and direct requests. Learning to ask for what you need, whether it's advice, connections, or resources, is crucial. Practice networking, and give as much as you receive to establish rapport and confidence.

- **Get vulnerable, create a founder council:** Building a business is not always smooth sailing. It's essential to be open about your struggles, even if you can't share them with investors or on social media. Find a trusted group of fellow founders who understand your challenges and can provide support and advice.

- **Get dangerous together:** Gaining technical skills, even basic ones, can be transformative for founders. Consider studying with another founder to enhance your technical proficiency. Whether through a coding bootcamp, or courses through our resource guide for this book, developing technical knowledge can significantly accelerate your journey.

- **Follow the GEMS framework:** This framework, introduced in the Chapters 2–6 of the book, provides a structured approach to building. Don't underestimate its effectiveness. Identify areas where you need support and seek out resources or individuals who can fill those gaps.

By adopting these strategies, we can work together, overcome barriers, and build a brighter future collectively. Although not every woman entrepreneur will ring the bell for an IPO, each one contributes to creating a more prosperous future. With gender disparities in data, funding, and technical skills, our unity becomes even more critical. The tools we need are at our disposal; we need only embrace them.

The Future Is Built Together

In closing, remember that the future is built collectively. As we traverse this new era of building, fueled by technology, we must remain committed to collaboration over competition. Let's continue to prioritize health, trust our instincts, and protect our energy.

Egos, although a natural part of human nature, should not hinder our progress. We are all vital components of this grand construction project, and our combined efforts will shape a brighter future. By following the seven strategies outlined here, we can build a network of support, seek alternative funding avenues, share mentor moments, perfect the art of the ask, become vulnerable, develop technical skills, and adhere to the GEMS framework.

As we build together, we strengthen our foundation and elevate ourselves. The future belongs to those who dare to dream, create, and collaborate. Together, we are architects of a brighter tomorrow, ready to craft a future where women lead, innovate, and inspire.

This is the future we're building, and it starts with you.

Code Review: Building Together for a Brighter Future

Congratulations on making it this far! You've now unlocked the power of collaboration in your journey as a builder of the future. Just like a well-structured code review, it's time to examine what you've learned and how you can apply it to your own life.

Founder Council Formation

Who are the potential members of your founder council?

Reflect on your network and think about individuals who share your values and are at similar stages in their entrepreneurial journey. Write down their names and consider reaching out to initiate discussions.

How can your founder council benefit you? Identify the specific challenges or areas where their insights could be most valuable. This could range from health and well-being to business strategies or tech-related issues.

Collaborative Opportunities

In which areas of your work could you benefit from collaboration with others?

Think about your current projects and endeavors. Are there aspects where teaming up with fellow entrepreneurs could lead to innovative solutions or shared knowledge?

What collaborative initiatives can you start or join within your industry or community?

Look for local meetups, online forums, or industry events where you can connect with like-minded individuals. Are there any existing groups you can contribute to or new ones you can create?

Ego Check

Reflect on a recent situation when you felt the need to protect your opportunities.

What motivated this reaction? Could collaboration have been a more beneficial approach in this instance?

How can you consciously set aside your ego in future business interactions?

Consider strategies for recognizing and mitigating the scarcity mindset when it arises, such as practicing gratitude or focusing on abundance.

The Power of Building Together

What resources, connections, or knowledge can you share with others in your industry or field?

Building a collaborative mindset means giving as well as receiving. Identify ways you can contribute to the success of fellow entrepreneurs. Consider mentorship, networking opportunities, or offering your expertise to bridge these divides.

Expanding Technical Skills

Reflect on the technical skills necessary for your entrepreneurial equation.

Are there specific areas where you could benefit from gaining more knowledge? Identify these areas and consider how acquiring these skills might empower your journey.

How can you collaborate with others to acquire technical skills?

Explore the possibility of forming study groups or participating in courses with fellow entrepreneurs. Share the learning process and accelerate your growth together.

The GEMS Framework

Assess your current strengths and weaknesses within the GEMS framework.

Which areas do you excel in, and where could you use improvement? This self-assessment will help you identify potential areas for collaboration and support. Maybe your marketing knowledge is lower in an area and you need more education. You could collaborate with someone who has more knowledge and share your expert knowledge with them on another area.

Remember, just as a code review enhances the quality of software, this reflection process will elevate your capacity to build a brighter future through collaboration and innovation. Keep your vision clear, your ambitions high, and your community close. Together, we're coding the future, one collaborative line at a time.

13

Testing the Vision

Before the Launch

Vision without execution is delusion.

—Thomas A. Edison

JUST LIKE THE final stages of crafting a groundbreaking product, realizing our vision of a future where women lead in innovation and tech requires thorough testing and fine-tuning. We've spent the preceding chapters developing this vision, gathering the lines of code of inspiration and knowledge, and programming them into a powerful concept. Now, as we stand on the verge of its launch, we must ensure it's ready for the world and to ensure that we, as the founders of this vision, are prepared for it to take off.

Imagine your vision for the future as a meticulously designed product. It's not enough to have an innovative concept; it must work flawlessly. This is where quality assurance comes into play for builders like us, signifying self-assessment. Are you ready to embrace the role of a builder in this vision? Have you truly absorbed the stories and knowledge shared here in this book?

It's like testing the user interface of your product to ensure it's intuitive and accessible.

Going through the quality assurance and testing process before launch is quite the process but it is important to look through each area that has been built, review the code, and make sure it is all working together. As this book comes to a close let's look back on our journey through these chapters, each one a distinct piece of the code to build the future.

I started the book with a glimpse into the future, a glimpse into the exciting possibilities of a future led by women in tech and innovation. We learned that innovation knows no gender boundaries and that we all have a role to play in shaping this future.

In Chapter 1, I shared my own journey into the world of tech and start-ups and laid the foundation for this book. We explored the power of stepping out of our comfort zones and embracing new opportunities like I did by going from the nonprofit sector into the tech and eventually entrepreneurship space.

In Chapter 2, I introduced you to the GEMS framework, which became our guiding star. We learned about the importance of grit, education, mindset, and support in our journey as builders. Frameworks like GEMS provide guidance and structure for personal and professional development. They can help you overcome self-doubt and excuses, fostering self-awareness and growth. This framework was laid out over the next few chapters and shares insights into my journey as a builder and how I overcame the hard days and made my entrepreneurial equation come to life.

In Chapter 3, I dove into grit and shared how you should think of your grit as a mental framework that embodies persistence and the will to overcome adversity. It's a skill that can be developed and refined over time, much like coding. I also hit on the dark side of grit and share that although grit is essential, it's crucial to recognize when you need a pause to avoid burnout. Balancing grit with self-care and acknowledging your limits is essential for long-term success.

In Chapter 4, we moved on to education, where I offer a comprehensive blueprint for those considering a career transition into the tech industry. It emphasizes the importance of self-assessment, mentorship, hands-on experience, documentation, and continuous learning. Additionally, it highlighted the role of AI tools such as ChatGPT in facilitating this transition, and set the stage for talking about how important technology is when building the future, which we dove more deeply into in Chapters 8 and 9.

In Chapter 5 we explored the concept of mindset within the context of personal and entrepreneurial development. I explain mindset to be a complex structure, much like a LEGO model, where each brick represents a belief or a lesson learned. Building a resilient mindset is crucial for success and I shared how you can program your mindset like you would code. In this chapter I also shared the parallels I found between learning to run and programming my mindset.

The last chapter of the GEMS framework, Chapter 6, focused on the importance of support in your building journey. I emphasized that support is not limited to professional networks but extends to all aspects of life, including personal relationships and self-motivation. The wonderful Hitha Palepu also shared her experience and knowledge on support in this chapter as well, and I pointed out one of my favorite resources for building your network, the book *Reach Out* by Molly Beck.

As we closed out the GEMS Framework we moved on to setting the stage for how we were going to take this framework and apply it to building the future. Chapter 7 discussed the concept of the entrepreneurial equation and how you can bring your passion together with technology to create impact and a brighter future. This chapter also shared the story of two technical women building a company together—Sara Mauskopf and Anne Halsall at Winnie—and the power and impact that two technical women building together can bring.

Chapter 8 took the reader into a journey of building and how to generate an idea for a start-up and make that idea a reality through planning out an MVP. This chapter gave you the knowledge and blueprint to start taking action on building the future now. But Chapter 9 went a step further and pushed you to get out of your comfort zone and get just dangerous enough when it comes to technology to be able to combine technology for forces of good in the world. These two chapters, paired with the GEMS framework, give you the tools and knowledge you need to make your entrepreneurial equation a reality.

Chapter 10 hit on the gaps that we encounter as women building the future, with gaps in data, care, and funding. The chapter shared my experience with those gaps and other founders that I interviewed on my podcast. The goal of this chapter is awareness so you have the information you need to conquer or work with the gaps.

As Chapter 11 drew the book closer to its conclusion, I share profiles and insights of women building the future. It's not just about my story; building the future requires all of us. My entrepreneurial equation is just one block in building the future; we need blocks in each industry to solve each problem our world faces. I am honored to be building alongside these amazing women and so many more are building or will start building who are not mentioned in this book.

Chapter 12 brought the book back around into maybe the most important lesson we all need to learn, and that is the value and importance of building together. We cannot build a brighter future alone; we need to work together to build that future and that takes putting our egos aside and bringing everyone along with us.

The Final Push

Before a product launch, there's a final push to polish every aspect. In our context, this translates to action. For me, what a journey this book has been to write and to share with each of you. As a builder and writer I know there are still final touches I will be putting on this book before it makes it into your hands one day, but I hope that as it is coming to an end you have found value and inspiration and that you feel excited and prepared to build the future. It's not enough to envision the future; we must actively participate in its creation. The chapters of this book have provided you with the tools and inspiration needed for this final push. Now, it's time to take what you've learned, combine it with your unique skills and perspective, and start building.

Ensuring a Smooth Launch

Just like a product launch, the realization of our vision should be smooth and impactful. We want it to capture attention, inspire change, and, most important, make a difference. This isn't a solo endeavor; it's a collaborative one. We're all in this together, testing, refining, and preparing for the grand launch.

So, as we approach the culmination of this transformative journey, remember that this is not the end; it's just the beginning of a new phase. We've tested our vision; now it's time to launch it into the world, together. Through collaboration, shared knowledge, and unwavering determination, we will turn this vision into a reality, just as a product becomes a reality in the hands of its users.

The ENIAC women, as we previously discussed, were foundational figures in the birth of computer programming. Their collaboration during World War II was pivotal, but the spirit of their teamwork didn't stop with them. The torch was passed on to other remarkable women in tech, like the indomitable Grace Hopper.

Rear Admiral Grace Hopper, often known as "Amazing Grace," is famed for her role in the development of the COBOL programming language and her work on the Harvard Mark I computer. But beyond her technical achievements, Grace was a fierce advocate for collaboration and mentorship. She believed that the best results came when diverse minds collaborated. Under her leadership, interdisciplinary teams flourished, combining the strengths of mathematicians, engineers, and even linguists.

I want to take a page out of Grace's playbook and pass the torch to each of you as this book comes to an end. It takes all of us to build a brighter future, and I have given you lots of tools, insight, and inspiration to go forth, but it is now time for you to take this further and share with others. We must join forces, set our egos aside, and bring our diverse talents together to build the future.

Manifesto

In the world of computer science, manifestos are powerful statements of principles and values that guide software development. They're blueprints for creating software that's efficient, reliable, and innovative. But today, we're not talking about code. We're talking about something even more transformative: building the future, not just with lines of code but with passion, purpose, and the indomitable spirit of women.

As you've journeyed through this book, you've encountered stories of resilience, ingenuity, and the relentless pursuit of dreams. Now, I present to you a different kind of manifesto, one that doesn't prescribe coding practices but lays out a road map for building the future together.

Building Tomorrow Together: The Future Built by Women

To every woman who has opened this book, to every dreamer who dares to envision a world steeped in innovation and goodness, this is for you.

From the stories shared and lessons imparted, you've embarked on a transformative journey through the pages of *The Future Built by Women*. Now, as you approach its end, it's essential to remember that every ending is a new beginning. You are on the precipice of a revolution, a future you have the power to shape.

Recall the GEMS
- **Grit:** Your resilience and determination will be the cornerstone of your success. When others see barriers, see bridges. Let setbacks become setups for future achievements.
- **Education:** Never stop learning. Dive deep into the ocean of knowledge, emerging as an empowered woman ready to make informed decisions and lead with wisdom.
- **Mindset:** Adopt a growth perspective. Understand that failure isn't the end, but a lesson. Celebrate your achievements, and more important, learn from your setbacks.
- **Support:** Lean on and be leaned on. We thrive most when we are together, supporting, uplifting, and inspiring one another. Community will be your greatest asset.

Embrace and Harness Technology
- **Connecting passion with technology:** Your passion is your compass, and technology, your ship. When fused together, they form a potent force that can create waves of change. Remember always to harness this power for good. Ensure that every tech-driven solution you birth is steeped in purpose and passion.
- **Be dangerously skillful:** You don't need to be an expert in everything, but equip yourself with just enough tech knowhow to be dangerous, dangerous enough to innovate, to disrupt, to lead.

Together We Go Further
- **Draw inspiration from others:** Every woman's success story you've read is proof that dreams, when combined with action, manifest into reality. Let their stories be the wind beneath your wings, urging you to soar higher.

- **Together we build:** Set aside ego. Embrace collaboration. Understand that our strengths—intuition, empathy, and patience—are potent tools. As women, we have the innate ability to nurture and build. Let's leverage these strengths to craft a brighter, inclusive, and equitable future.

Action Steps for You

- **Find your council:** Surround yourself with like-minded women. Build, fail, and succeed together.
- **Educate daily:** Dedicate some time each day to learn something new, however small, about technology and innovation.
- **Challenge yourself:** Step out of your comfort zone regularly. Attend tech events, engage in buildathons, or simply brainstorm innovative solutions for everyday problems.
- **Mentor and be mentored:** The cycle of learning never stops. As you ascend, pull others up with you. And as you learn, teach.
- **Celebrate every milestone:** Big or small, every step forward is progress.

Believe in yourself, in the strength of sisterhood, and in the promise of a future where technology and goodness coexist. Go forth and be the beacon, for the future built by women starts with you.

A Thank-You

Thank you for being a part of this incredible journey. The future is ready to be built, and we're the ones to build it, collaboratively and with boundless ambition. Let's step into this future and make it the reality we've envisioned, and then some.

The Built x Women Resource Guide

THIS GUIDE WILL evolve over time as the future of technology evolves, so check back often. The goal of this guide is to make sure you have all the resources that have supported me in building the future. I spent a lot of hours and years finding the best resources and have curated this source for you. I have split it up into sections based on the GEMS framework so you can lean into areas you are lacking and to help you swoop in and grab what you need when you need it. You can access the guide at www.thefu turebuiltbywomen.com.

How best to use this guide:

- Identify what you need most right now to move your business or idea forward, or to help your mindset if you are struggling.
- Choose that section and explore.
- Still not sure? Email us at team@builtxwomen.com so our team can make a suggestion.

Acknowledgments

WRITING A BOOK is much like writing code. It starts with an initial spark, a blueprint of what one hopes to achieve. Along the way, there are bugs to fix, endless iterations, and continuous refining. But what truly elevates any code—or book—are the collaborators who bring their unique expertise to the project. In the coding journey of this book, I have been graced with an extraordinary team.

Edgar, you have been my primary debugger, always there to help troubleshoot life's challenges, optimize my routines, and enhance my vision's UI/UX. With every early morning writing session and MVP launch, your unwavering support was the framework on which this project ran smoothly.

Lily, you have been my intuitive algorithm, guiding my logic and infusing it with creativity. Your innate ability to craft stories has been an inspiration, pushing me to code a brighter future for you. Lukas, my little beta tester, your curiosity and joy have been the patches that often resolved my life's unexpected bugs.

Chloe, as the COO of Allobee, not only were you my fellow architect, understanding the intricacies of our mission's blueprint

221

and ensuring our platform's seamless functionality, but also a cherished friend whose camaraderie made the journey even more rewarding (thank you for hopping on that flight to San Diego!). Niki, as our first engineering hire, each line of code we built together was a stepping stone in realizing our vision, and I cannot thank you enough. Heather, throughout the acquisition and beyond, your insights and friendship have been a grounding constant, guiding and enlightening my path. Kesa, your encouragement served as the "code comments" in my narrative, and our friendship provided warmth and clarity, ensuring that I kept the code clean and efficient.

To every member of The Hive at Allobee: thanks to each one of you, we constructed a digital ecosystem where women are recognized and rewarded for their flexible contributions.

A heartfelt thank-you to all the women I had the privilege of interviewing for this book. Your insights, experiences, and visions were the unique functions that added depth and perspective to this narrative. Each of you exemplifies the spirit of a builder, coding a more inclusive and innovative future.

Dreamers and doers, your platform was the interface that connected my vision to Wiley, leading me down the path to a dream realized.

Adaobi, in the realm of this book's code, you've been my meticulous code reviewer, ensuring that each line resonated with its intended function. Victoria, your unwavering belief in this project was the motivational plug-in I needed, and to the entire Wiley team, thank you for deploying this project to its best version.

To my family, your enduring support has been the foundational code on which I've built. Your faith in my visions and dreams, and the space you've always given me to be myself, have been invaluable. You've provided the unshakable base on which I've been able to envisage and build not only for myself but also for countless others.

And to you, dear readers, thank you for taking the time to read this book and for exploring how you can become "dangerous enough" and build a brighter future for us all.

In the vast domain of tech and innovation, every coder knows the significance of collaboration. This book is the culmination of collective efforts, each one of you being an indispensable line of code in its structure. Together, we've coded a brighter, innovative future, and for that my gratitude runs endless loops.

About the Author

Brooke Markevicius, a recognized start-up product leader and keynote speaker, is celebrated for her keen insights and mission-driven leadership. Transitioning from the nonprofit sector, she harnessed tech to effect meaningful change. While balancing her roles as a mom of two and founder of the innovative start-up Allobee, Brooke guided the platform to a notable acquisition. Featured in *Forbes*, *Fast Company*, and more, she ardently champions women in tech and entrepreneurship. She now resides in Durham, North Carolina, where she harnesses technology for profound good and invites women to combine passion with technology, forging a future where women lead with assurance.

Index